HOW TO PERFECT YOUR GOLF SWING

USING 'CONNECTION' AND THE SEVEN COMMON DENOMINATORS

BY JIMMY BALLARD

WITH BRENNAN QUINN
ILLUSTRATED BY JIM McQUEEN
FOREWORD BY JOHN BRODIE

A
GOLF
DIGEST
BOOK

Distributed by:
Golf Digest/Tennis, Inc.
A New York Times Company
5520 Park Avenue
Post Office Box 0395
Trumbull, CT 06611-0395

Trade book distribution by
Simon and Schuster
A Division of Simon & Schuster, Inc.
Rockefeller Center
1230 Avenue of the Americas
New York, New York 10020

Manufactured in the United States of America
Printing and binding by R.R. Donnelley & Sons.
Cover and book design by Dorothy Geiser.
Typesetting by J&J Typesetters, Norwalk, Connecticut

Library of Congress Cataloging-in-Publication Data

Ballard, Jimmy.
   How to perfect your golf swing.

   "A Golf Digest book."
   1. Swing (Golf)   I. Quinn, Brennan.   II. Title.
   [GV979.S9B34 1986]   796.352'3   86-186
ISBN 0-914178-83-0 (pbk.)

DEDICATION:
To my wife, Pat, and my
daughters, Kim and Kellye.

ACKNOWLEDGEMENTS: | Many people contributed to the making of this book, more than can be acknowledged here. But special thanks are due to Billy MacDonald, Lee Mackey, Mac McLendon, John Brodie, Bruce Devlin, Fred Erben, the late John P. Moss, and the late Sam Byrd.

PHOTO CREDITS: | Lester Nehamkin, 38 (left); Jack Scagnetti, 38 (right), 125; Steve Szurlej, 62, 63, 114; John P. May, 84, 159; Tony Roberts, 95; John Newcomb, 149-55 (Littler sequence); Golf Digest, 149-55 (Nicklaus sequence), 157

TABLE OF CONTENTS

FOREWORD

For the past several years, Jimmy Ballard has had extraordinary results as an instructor working with touring professionals as well as recreational golfers of all ability levels. And a careful reading of this new book will make the reasons readily apparent. With the help of Brennan Quinn, he has presented his unique teaching principles so that the reader is taken swiftly along a route to a refreshingly clear understanding of the golf swing. Confusion is erased once the reader comprehends and applies Jimmy's concept of "connection" and the seven common denominators—seven simple truths that, in fact, are directly tied to successful performance in many areas of athletic endeavor.

Golf is nothing if it's not fun. Personally, I've experienced Jimmy as a high-spirited southerner, an involved family man, a great teacher, a fabulous host and above all, a good friend. Jimmy approaches the game seriously, but he knows the positive lasting efforts of lower handicaps and scores. For those of you who both enjoy the game and seek improvement, I heartily recommend this book.

—John Brodie, TV sports commentator,
former pro football star

INTRODUCING JIMMY BALLARD

Jimmy Ballard, the man Frank Beard has predicted will be "the most sought after golf instructor in the world in the 1980's," has been teaching golfers essentially the same approach for the past two decades. Where did it all begin?

In 1956, as a 14-year-old resident of Gadsden, Alabama, Jimmy won the state amateur golf championship in his age group. But that fall, the family moved to Birmingham and he enrolled at Woodlawn High School. At the time, Woodlawn featured state championship teams in two sports—football and basketball. Golf was considered somewhat of a geriatric endeavor, and Ballard was not one to miss out on the action favored by his peers. The pride of Woodlawn deposited his clubs in the closet and spent the next three years in a world of hoops, hardwood, hip pads, and hyperextended ligaments. During fall football practice of his senior year, a foot injury forced him off the gridiron and, while recuperating, he hauled his dust-laden golf clubs out from behind the family Hoover.

He shot a 69 the first time he played after a three-year layoff and thought "Hell! This game just isn't that hard," but within a week, he needed chip-ins to break 80: it had become obvious to him that he didn't know what he was doing regardless of how he played or scored.

The year was 1960. A friend referred him to one Sam Byrd, owner of and teaching professional at a driving range in the Crestwood section of Birmingham. In 1978, at age 72, Sam had retired as head pro at the Anniston (Ala.) C.C. following a distinguished career as a baseball player in the majors (1929-1936, including shagging flies alongside of Babe Ruth with the Yankees) and a touring golf pro who won over 25 events, finished third in both the 1941 and 1942 Masters, and was the runner-up to Byron Nelson in the 1945 PGA Championship.

Byrd had spent a lifetime mining the mysteries of the correct application of hickory to horsehide, and then that of persimmon to balata. In Ballard he quickly perceived a man with an insatiable curiosity about the golf swing, and also one with no aversion to hard work. The upshot was that Sam Byrd hired Ballard as his assistant.

Ballard proved to be an extremely quick study—one of those rare individuals who knew that to be an effective teacher you have to be a precise communicator. In 1965, when Byrd returned to a club position, Jimmy took over his range operation. Ever since then, Ballard has continued to acknowledge the golf legacy left him by the man he calls "The Alabama Yankee."

"Basically I'm teaching the same fundamentals today that Sam introduced me to twenty years ago," says Ballard, "with the only difference being I have evolved my own way of communicating them."

In a short time, Jimmy achieved a reputation for remarkable success in teaching local amateurs and word spread quickly that here was someone who could make a lasting change for the better in a hacker's golf swing. In 1972, he set up shop at Pine Harbor C.C., near Pell City, about 50 miles from Birmingham, and soon began entertaining swing-stricken visitors from the PGA and LPGA tours.

The first of these was Mac McLendon, referred by a local banker friend whose own amateur golf game had been much enhanced by the Ballard treatment. When McLendon's performance on tour skyrocketed the roof about caved in. Since then more than a hundred professionals have visited with Jimmy.

What about the style and content of Jimmy's teaching?

Let me take you through an abbreviated version of a

typical day with Jimmy Ballard, golf professional. I think it will help you better appreciate the Ballard instructional message which follows.

Tuesday through Saturday, lessons begin at 9 a.m., as golf cars roll away from the pro shop, speed through the parking lot, and then wind across the first and ninth fairways toward the practice area. The procession of staff and students is led by Ballard himself who rides shotgun to a high-priced video pack and the sequence camera on the seat next to him.

On the practice tee, Ballard first asks his golfers to warm up by hitting a few balls with a medium or short iron. He chats briefly with the players on the line— "What's your handicap?" "Where do you play?", etc.,— light conversation designed to offset the mild nervousness or tension that players often experience in starting a day-long lesson.

After the golfers have hit enough balls to ensure that this morning's swing shape is reasonably close to the normal playing patterns, Jimmy moves his videomobile into position and "shoots" each student. Several sequences are shot straight on—facing the golfer—and several from behind, down the intended line of flight. As he's looking through his lens, Jimmy is apt to query, "Do you shove a lot of shots to the right?" or, "Hit most of your irons fat on a bad day—especially long irons?" "Yes" is the usual answer, and the reply to that, inevitably, is, "Well, we'll take care of that!"

But during this general warmup and recording phase of the day, that's the extent of the conversation. At this stage, the golfers receive no verbal instructions or physical demonstrations.

Once the video tape is in the can, Jimmy asks those students who are taking their first lesson from him to return to their golf cars and follow him back toward the pro shop and lodge. He leads his small armada back over the two fairways, through the parking lot, past the pro shop, and stops at the bottom of the stairway that leads up to a room on the second story of the lodge.

Antique clubs and pictures of the touring pros who visit Pine Harbor adorn the wood-panelled and used-brick walls. There is a large sofa, tables and side chairs, Franklin stove, small desk, and a monitoring screen and tape deck. A vast collection of sequence photos, gathered by Jimmy over the years, and protected by clear plastic covers, is strewn on one of the tables.

When all students are seated, the instruction begins. Essentially, the teaching is separated into four basic areas of discussion:

1) The terms used to teach the golf swing that Ballard thinks are misleading
2) The fundamentals, or common denominators, that Ballard thinks are present in the swings of all great strikers of the ball
3) The teaching of 'feel' through various drills and exercises
4) The application of everything discussed to each individual's swing.

All of these areas are treated in the course of the text which follows. For now, let me relate one golfer's experiences and observations, in the hope that it will provide you, the reader, with a personal look at the way Ballard teaches.

Jimmy began with me by talking about my address position, specifically about the position of my legs. He first showed me how he thought I looked, and then demonstrated how I should consider changing. Turning on the tape machine he showed me at address, freezing that position on the screen. He then took photographs of Hogan, Snead, Nicklaus and Weiskopf, lay them in front of me and asked that I study their address positions, comparing them to mine as it appeared on the monitor. He then asked a question he asks many times in a lesson situation, "Do you see that?"

In day to day conversation, when we ask that question of someone, we simply mean, "Do you get it?" This is not the question Ballard is asking. He is trying to find out if you visually appreciate the differences and to confirm this, he may ask you to explain what you see. Once this has been done, he'll tell you how the difference you both have agreed exists, adversely affects your swing. Following such an explanation, Ballard will probe, "Am I confusing you in any way?" or "Does that make sense to you?" Clearly, he is wary of the possibility of communication breakdowns.

My poor address position was easy for me to see, and the opportunity to sit and study the differences between my position and the position of the "great ball strikers," side by side, etched it even more clearly in my mind. Jimmy went on to point out that partly because of the problem just discussed, I was not able to coil into the strongest possible position at the top of my swing. He ran the tape ahead, and stopped my swing at the top. At that point I was again asked to 'visually appreciate' the difference achieved by Hogan, Snead and Nicklaus. I was allowed sufficient time to study the differences and I saw that these other fellows were coiled deeper behind the ball. I, on the other hand, had pirouetted and remained more or less over the ball. It's refreshing to be able to compare the position you achieve at a particular point in the swing with positions achieved by the greatest golfers that have ever played. Long ago I became convinced that in anything that has to do with movement sport, my eyes and body are smarter than my mind. Anyway, Ballard had given me a 'mind's eye' frame of reference for my address position that I would not soon forget. I was not about to contest the fact. Hogan, Snead, Nicklaus and Ballard had me closed out!

Ballard next suggested, "It looks like we've got to get you in a better position behind the ball," and talked about how my present position prevented me from moving properly into the impact area and on through to a balanced finish. While he stressed that we were only going to work on two things that day—the position of my legs at address, and achieving the desired position behind the ball—he wanted me to understand how these had to be integrated into the total swing. "We can't ever work on more than two things at one time," he said. "Correct these two, and the other elements will begin to fall into place. As we progress, we'll tie in the rest!"

Ballard then gave me some analagous moves related to other sports to help cement my idea of what I was attempting to do. "I don't think the hard part is understanding," he said. "The real trick is finding an individual's particular 'feel' for the move we are trying to impart. We might try six different ways to get you behind the ball until we hit on a verbal or visual chord that has resonance for you and therefore works."

Jimmy worked with me for a while and then had his assistants continue the good fight. Last time I saw him, after I had hit perhaps my 1,001th range ball into the receding sunset, he came over to ask, "You're sure you are not confused about anything we've discussed?"

I told him I wasn't.

CHAPTER ONE

'CONNECTION' AND THE SEVEN COMMON DENOMINATORS

Connection In All Sports

Good athletes in all sports use the entire body in a manner that produces the most effective and visually pleasing combination of power, accuracy and grace. Connection refers to the natural sequential wholeness and efficiency of their actions, and it invariably involves the use of the large muscles of the body. Whether it's Willie Mays in baseball, Rod Laver in tennis, Terry Bradshaw in football or Jack Nicklaus in golf, the best exponents of athletic achievement operate from the ground up through body center, and never depend solely on the smaller muscles in their hands and arms.

Twenty years ago, when I decided to become a teacher, it became obvious to me that any success I might achieve would be based upon two prerequisites. First, progress would depend on my discovering the true fundamentals in the golf swing, and with these essential principles established, step two would involve devising and testing a sound method of communicating these principles—a teaching method which produced the desired results with every student who was willing to apply some diligence. At the risk of sounding immodest, I believe my method of teaching has assisted some of professional golf's finest players, male and female, and perhaps even more satisfying, has turned some near self-destructive hackers into solid golfing citizens with only one number next to their names on the club handicap board. I have chosen to devote my working life to this task, and my many pleasant experiences with the games of thousands of golfers convince me that I can do the same with you.

But let us be realistic at the outset. Three years ago, John Schroeder first came to see me. To be very honest, and John will agree, at this point he was a basket case. I told him at the time that we had a number of changes to make; that it would be at least two years before he should expect to win a tournament, but that in a matter of weeks he would be able to make money on the tour. John and I worked hard together, and since that first meeting he has won well over $300,000.

The interesting thing about making a statement in the form of a rule is that it is invariably followed by an exception. In May of 1978, Jim Simons came for help. Within two weeks, he won Jack Nicklaus' tournament at Muirfield—nosing out another exceptional player I've had the privilege of working with, Bill Kratzert. In light of the swing changes Jim and I discussed, that win was a truly outstanding feat.

Another gratifying experience has been working with Curtis Strange, who came to see me initially in April of 1980 and has returned periodically to check his progress. By combining talent, intelligence, a rapid learning ability, and dedication, he improved his fundamentals immediately and at this time he is one of the premier professional golfers in the world.

I will always carry fond memories of 1979. For me, that was definitely the year of the woman. In about a six-month period, I worked with Jan Ferraris, Alice Ritzman, Jane Blalock, Sylvia Bertolaccini, Penny Pulz and Jerilyn Britz. All improved. Blalock won four tournaments, while Bertolaccini, Pulz and Britz all won their first tour events—Britz in the U.S. Open. In my opinion, these successes were predicated upon a willingness to make necessary changes and stay with them. Those mentioned gave up "try this—try that" golf and got back to consistently working on the same fundamental considerations. Their patience and perseverance paid off.

Quite frankly, a swing change, even when a player is totally convinced of the necessity, is not always a comfortable process. New movement, like the patience needed to produce it repeatedly, is an acquired virtue. It's not easy to unlearn old habits, and before changes are assimilated, it's only human nature to fall back on what's familiar and comfortable—particularly under pressure. Lee Trevino readily admits to hitting a thousand balls a day for five years, and Ben Hogan's swing changes were not the product of some overnight revelation. It's kind of a two-steps-forward, one-step-back proposition for most players. But if we are trying to achieve permanent improvement, some temporary discomforts are the dues that must be paid. Let me hasten to say that I'm not trying to frighten you, but only to be truthful. I know it works, and what I'll suggest to you now is this: Read this book carefully. Take your time, and digest the material step by step. If you'll stay with it, I won't guarantee you'll win the club championship in two years, but I will give you four to one that in the near future, your opponents will get tired of paying your green fees and bar bills.

My teaching approach is founded upon a number of fundamentals I refer to as the common denominators in the golf swing. Quite simply, the common denominators are the identifiable essential movements that appear in the swings of all of the great ball strikers past and present. Let me make one important distinction. There is a difference between a great ball striker and a great player. There have been a number of great players who didn't consistently strike the ball that well, but managed through competitive tenacity and intelligent on-course management to enjoy some measure of success. As tournament golfers, however, almost without exception, their careers ended prematurely—their games lacked the fundamental soundness necessary for longevity.

The great ball strikers, on the other hand, are those individuals who have continued to be successful in the crucible of competition for an extended period of time —Hogan, Snead, Nelson, Boros, Littler and Nicklaus, to mention but a few.

My teaching premise is simple. Whether a person

wishes to pursue golf as a profession or as a lifelong recreational endeavor, the answers to the questions concerning how to strike a golf ball properly must reside in the time-tested swings of the great ball strikers. Where else could they be? Viewed objectively, and stripped of unnecessary elaboration, there are basically seven things that all of the great ball strikers do in common. In this book, as I do in a lesson situation, I am going to focus on these seven elements. The book contains visual aids in the form of photos and artwork drawn precisely from photos of the great ball strikers exhibiting to perfection the seven common denominators. Beyond these, the differences in swing are matters of individual mannerism or style.

At this time, I will not list the seven because the list includes some terminology yet unfamiliar to you, and would consequently be of little value now. But, speaking in capsule form for the moment, I defy anyone to show me that all the great ball strikers did not: (1) coil behind the ball on the backswing, (2) hit through it—and past it (3) into a straight balanced finish. I know that sounds easy, and frankly, the golf swing isn't as difficult as almost everyone wants to make it.

CONNECTION—SPORT'S MASTER FUNDAMENTAL

As a young teacher, I spent countless hours trying to find a way to communicate to my students the natural, sequential wholeness or the unified efficiency of the actions that I could plainly see in the swings of all of the great ball strikers. In fact, my observations were not limited to golf. I could see the same unified quality of movement exhibited in the performances of top-level athletes in all sports. It became obvious that these indi-

---

Feeling Connection In Golf

Here's a simple drill for immediately acquiring the feeling of connection in the golf swing. Stand in your normal address position holding something fairly heavy such as a shag bag full of balls, a medicine ball or the like, and try throwing it with some authority toward a target about 15 feet away, as shown. You will discover that to do this effectively you will naturally draw on the large muscles in your legs and back. To have a powerful golf swing, your whole body has to get into the act. If you rely primarily on your hands and arms to toss the shag bag, or to swing a golf club, you'll lose both power and accuracy.

viduals had learned to use the entire anatomy in a manner that produced the most effective and visually pleasing combination of power, accuracy and grace. Such a sight once prompted a spectator to observe: "Watching Sam Snead practice short irons is like watching a fish practice swimming!" A spectator could satisfy his compulsion to share an experience with a friend by talking of ease, timing, smoothness, rhythm or tempo. But these are fiendish words to the serious teacher. How can I teach you rhythm in an hour with any assurance that what I provide will be retained? I probably can't! It's like the little boy who, fascinated by the wind, runs outside and traps some in a shoe box, only to return to his room, open the box, and find nothing but stillness.

Obviously, trying to constantly redefine these same old "airy" golf terms was not the answer. How then could I reduce this visual wholeness to something that would capture the essence, and also provide me with a tool to communicate and build this efficiency of motion into the swing of a student?

The word I found was "connection." The physical activity of any top level athlete was connected, as opposed to being a disjointed or disconnected action. And it seemed to me to be particularly apparent in any of the striking or stick-and-ball sports. Whether the athlete was swinging a club, racquet, bat or paddle, the very best players controlled the hands and arms with the big muscles of the body—the large muscles of the legs, torso and shoulders—rather than with the smaller muscles of the arms and hands. Proper utilization of the body initially produced the power which was then transmitted through the arms and hands. Never the reverse! It was particularly noticeable in golf, and the evidence was quite simple. All poor golfers were arm- and hand-dominant, and all great ball strikers were not. The average player was allowing the tail to wag the dog. The great ball strikers all had the dog wagging the tail!

In my teaching, the idea of connection became the master fundamental. It was not at all complicated, and I didn't really consider it as either theory or concept. It was an observable physical reality—what was actually happening in the best golf swings. Initially, connection was made up of grip, position and balance, and a connected golf swing possessed all of the common denominators—the essential fundamentals. In other words, connection was introduced into the player's set-up and maintained throughout the swing by the presence and sequential continuance of the fundamentals. Any fundamental departure was a disconnection which interrupted the correct interrelationships. This made it possible to view the whole swing as connected and the parts as elements of connection. The process begins by teaching a student the braced connected address position. From there, we proceed to each of the fundamentals (the common denominators) as they appear from the time the player swings the club away from the ball, until he reaches the straight balanced finish. At this point, the golfer should understand the essential elements of the connected golf swing. Then, with some application, the player can train his golfing dog to wag his golfing tail and perhaps enjoy one of man's best pastimes for the first time in his life.

Suppose I ask you to assume your normal address position, standing sideways to an open door or window some 15 feet away, holding a shag bag full of practice balls in front of you. Now I ask you to hurl the shag bag through the window with some authority.

How would you naturally perform this action? Let me answer that for you, describing what you would do in some detail, not because I expect you to be consciously aware of these details during such an action—quite the contrary—but simply to familiarize you with golf's master fundamental a little better.

With the weight equally distributed on the insides of your feet and legs, you could coil the entire upper body, the hands, arms, shoulders and torso together, against what I call a brace or set of the right leg. In the process, the head moves marginally to the right, simply following the spine.

As the bag reaches a point just above waist level going back, your weight moves onto the inside of the right foot and right leg, and your point of balance is six to eight inches behind the mid-line of your body.

From here, you reverse the thrust of the legs from the ground up. Since the weight is predominantly "loaded" on the inside of the right foot, leg and hip joint, you must start the weight transfer from there with a thrust of the right foot and right knee combined, followed immediately by a thrust of the whole right side, upper body, arms and hands.

With this thrust or kick of the right foot and knee, your point of balance shifts to the left foot some six to eight inches in front of the mid-line of your body. Having accomplished this, your left side clears to accommodate the weight transfer and your arms are now swinging directly toward your target.

As you release the shag bag, your hands are pointing at the open window, your weight is almost totally on the left foot, your hips and shoulders are level, and the head and eyes are up, tracking the bag to its destination.

In this way, you have thrown the shag bag properly,

using natural rhythm and coordination in a totally connected tossing action. It is precisely the action present in
the swing of every great striker of the ball, past, present
and future.

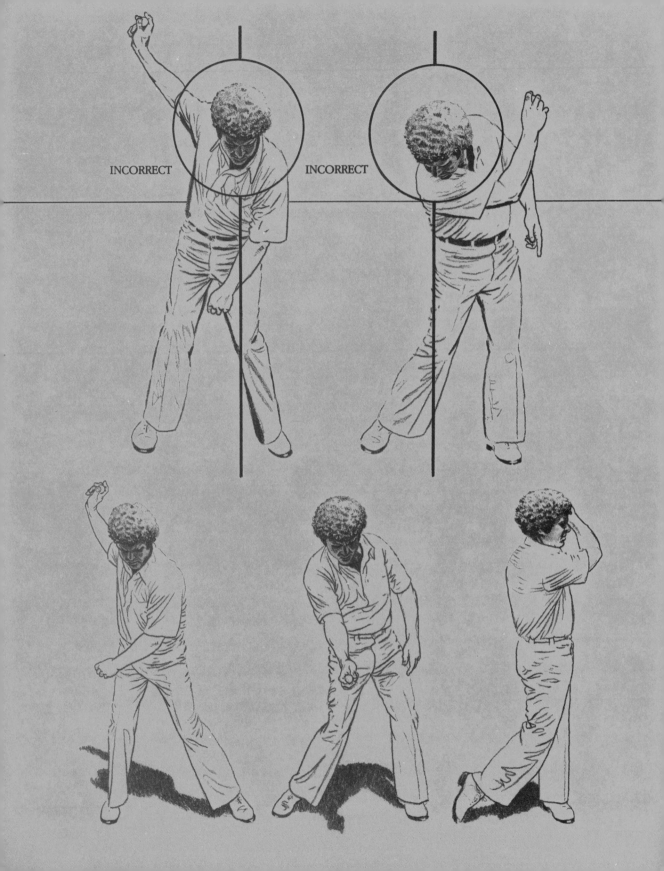

INCORRECT INCORRECT

CHAPTER TWO

GOLF'S MISLEADING TERMS

Misleading Terms: "Keep Your Head Down (Or Still)"

If you try to lock your head into position as this misleading term suggests, you'll tend to shift into a reverse pivot on your backswing and you'll inhibit your finish on the follow-through. The head must flow with the spine during the golf swing if you are to generate any real power. The head does not pull the body. Try throwing a ball sidearm from your normal address position, as depicted in the sequence, and you'll get an accurate feeling for the range of permissible and necessary head movement in the golf swing.

Before discussing the common denominators with my students, I always find it helpful to treat in detail what I call the misleading terms in the golf swing. I stress six of them, and if the reader has ever taken a golf lesson or digested any instructional material, they will be familiar. My experience has convinced me that use of these terms often prevents players from employing the natural and fundamental moves essential to good golf. Each one—by itself—can literally destroy the golfer's potential if he or she persists in using it as a conscious swing key.

Neither I nor my teaching professionals ever utter one of these terms in the course of a lesson. After we have concluded the following section I'm going to ask you also to delete them from your golfing vocabulary once and for all. As we unlearn the terms, and rid ourselves of any initial fear we might have in proceeding without them, we'll break down the first barriers to better golf. Clearing our minds of the excess baggage is the first step toward an accurate and comfortable comprehension of the true fundamentals in the golf swing.

Keeping the head down. Undoubtedly, the oldest and most sacred admonition in the game of golf is: Keep your head down. As a conscious swing key, it is also one of the most dangerous. If you try to lock your head into position as this term suggests, you'll tend to shift into a reverse pivot on your backswing and you'll inhibit your finish on the follow through. The head must move with the spine during the swing if you are to generate any real power.

Try throwing a ball sidearm from your normal address position and you'll get an accurate feeling for the range of permissible and necessary head movement in

INCORRECT

Misleading Terms:
"Keep Your Left Arm
Straight (Or Stiff)"

Not only does this mis-
leading term generate
unwanted tension in the
swing, but it produces almost
immediate disconnection on
the backswing. Notice how in
the incorrect backswing
example, the left arm has
stretched away from the
chest. From this position the
arms will have to pull the
club back down to the ball
with little help from the
major body muscles.

the golf swing. Trying to hold the head down or still destroys the natural rhythm and coordination of the body. In the golf swing, the player must treat the head the same way he would while pitching a ball sidearm. He must learn to let it move naturally with the spine, and allow the head and eyes to track the shot.

A conscious attempt to keep the head down restricts the shoulders and upper body and actually promotes dipping. Later, we will discuss the permissible latitude as to head movement in detail. But for the moment, the point is this: If "head down" has been one of your swing thoughts, dismiss it, without being afraid of the consequences.

"Moving off the ball" is the delinquent brother of "Keeping the head down" or "still." Almost without exception, golfers have been brainwashed into having an inordinate fear of what they conceive to be a "sway" or "move off the ball." As in the shag bag tossing ex- ample, if a person is simply going to stand flatfooted and "twist" or turn the body, rather than coiling back into a natural position, he'll have nothing to throw or hit with except the hands and arms.

A player must learn the difference between a move off the ball and the proper move behind the ball, which will also be discussed in detail later. For now, we don't want you to be afraid of moving, because until this indoctri- nated bias has been erased, it will be impossible to learn to coil into your strongest and most natural backswing position.

Stiff left arm. In any of the sports in which a player is trying to advance an object with a club, bat, racquet, paddle or stick, live, supple but essentially *soft* arms are an absolute must. It should be obvious to most readers that stiffness at any point in the golf swing creates unwanted tension and restriction which robs the player of both power and accuracy.

Hand- and arm-dominance is the arch-enemy of the average golfer. We will see that the great strikers in golf initiate the swing from the ground up, and therefore in reality swing the arms with the body. After we have discussed the proper "connected" left arm, and explained correct extension, it will be clear that conscious tightening of the left arm restricts the legs and torso, destroying a player's natural rhythm and coordination.

Dismiss your inclinations for preserving a stiff left arm. Arms and hands never dominate in golf, but react reflexively to the connected releasing of the entire body.

Pulling down with the back of the left hand or the butt of the club. Other familiar instructions, such as trying to preserve the wrist cock or creating the late hit also fall into this category. Several years ago, with the advent of stop-action photography, it became possible to freeze the motion in movement sport. Unfortunately for a number of teachers and players alike, this advancement became a step backward. People began trying to isolate and intentionally re-create parts of the golf swing in which the club was traveling close to 100 mph. If the club is traveling that fast, it's a result or an effect, it *can't* be a cause. In my estimation, trying to teach such a "position" is an impossibility.

A golfer destroys his chances of consistently squaring up to the ball at impact by making a conscious effort to pull down with the back of the left hand or the butt of the club. Suppose you were going to back-hand something that was in front of you, just below your waist, approximately in the position your hands would be in if you were striking a golf ball. You wouldn't consciously make an attempt to pull your left arm downward. If you

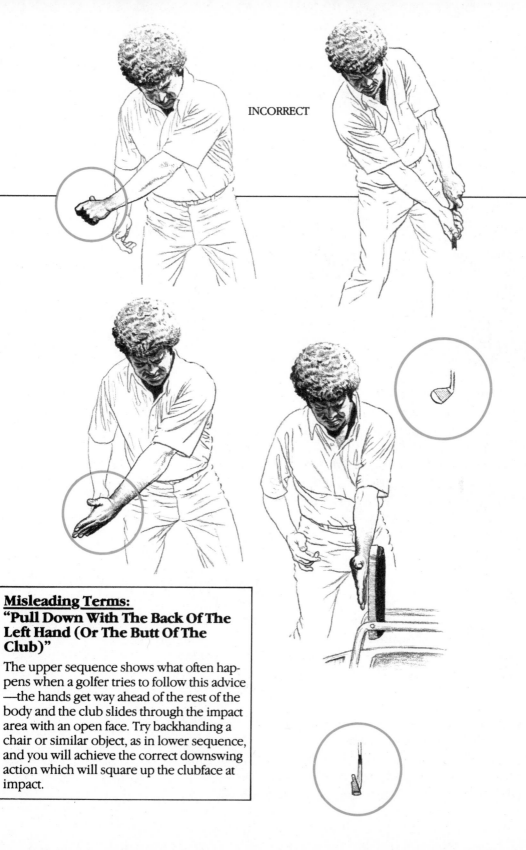

INCORRECT

Misleading Terms:
"Pull Down With The Back Of The Left Hand (Or The Butt Of The Club)"

The upper sequence shows what often happens when a golfer tries to follow this advice—the hands get way ahead of the rest of the body and the club slides through the impact area with an open face. Try backhanding a chair or similar object, as in lower sequence, and you will achieve the correct downswing action which will square up the clubface at impact.

did, chances are you'd make contact with the butt of your hand.

Golfers are sometimes confused as to the difference between the back of the hand and the butt of the hand, or what's commonly referred to as the heel of the hand. If you are wearing a golf glove, the trademark is on the back of the hand. Presuming a proper grip, the clubface cannot be squared up at impact until the trademark is facing the target. As long as the golfer makes a conscious effort to pull down with the butt of the club, or the back of the left hand, the trademark will be facing skyward and the clubface will remain open.

Never dwell on any of these "pull down" or "late hit" instructions, because in point of fact, the left arm works sideways and squares up to the ball as opposed to working down. If you have keyed on any of these terms as swing thoughts, I'm going to ask you to dismiss them from your golfing memory bank.

Staying behind the ball. Once again, let's imagine that you are going to toss a shag bag through a door as you did in the "head down" discussion. If you tried to throw the ball while making a conscious effort to "stay back," what would happen? Presuming you coiled back into a natural throwing position, in a concentrated attempt to stay there, you would spin or twist, leaving the weight on the right foot, and releasing the bag to the left of the door into the wall. Even if by chance you happened to time your release of the bag and toss it through the door, it would be a matter of luck, because the path of your arms would not be swinging in the direction of your target, but to the left of it.

The golf swing should approximate the natural tossing motion, so that you feel your way through the door, or down the intended target line. Any attempt to key on

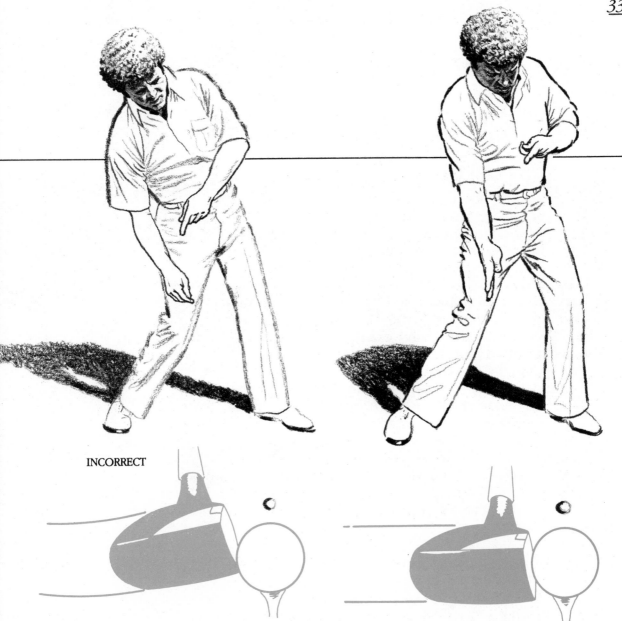

INCORRECT

Misleading Terms: **"Stay Behind The Ball"**

This term promotes falling back with thin or topped shots a frequent result. The large muscles of legs and body are not allowed to play their part in driving through the ball. There's a tendency to hit under and up instead of down and through when one strives to "stay behind the ball."

"staying behind" or "back" of the ball will ultimately deaden legs and body, thus destroying the natural rhythm and coordination of the swing.

Turn. On my lesson tee, a player might occasionally hear some four-letter words, but if one of them is "turn," it has not been uttered by my assistants or myself. I imagine that most golfers would think it impossible to teach the game without using the word turn. On the contrary, I've found that it's next to impossible to teach golf properly if you do! In my experience, emphasizing a turn or turning prevents 95 percent of golfers from employing their natural rhythm and coordination. Turning as a swing thought or key causes players to twist their bodies, rather than produce the sufficient, natural lateral movement of the weight back and through. Later, we will see that turning from two joints that are anatomically affixed to each other (pelvis and hip joints) is a practical impossibility. Let's disregard the words turn and turning and replace them with more accurate descriptions of what happens in a proper golf swing, namely, the proper "coil" or the coiling and recoiling sensations.

Hitting into the "reverse C finish" or "bow" position. During the last few years, due in part to the general acceptance by instructors of the incorrect notion that their students should exaggerate the attempt to stay behind the ball, players have tried to finish the swing with the head approximately over the right foot and the right shoulder under the left. To the untrained eye, this appeared to be athletic-looking—even graceful. It's wonderful if a player enjoys topping shots and inviting lower back problems. As we shall see, all of the great ball strikers finish with the shoulders level, in a posture best described as a straight balanced finish. If a

---

> **Misleading Terms: "Turn"**
>
> The trouble with this term is that it encourages golfers to twist into what amounts to a reverse pivot rather than coiling back into a natural and powerful backswing position. If you stood on one leg, flamingo-style, you could turn on the single hip joint. But the golf swing is made from both hip joints.

INCORRECT

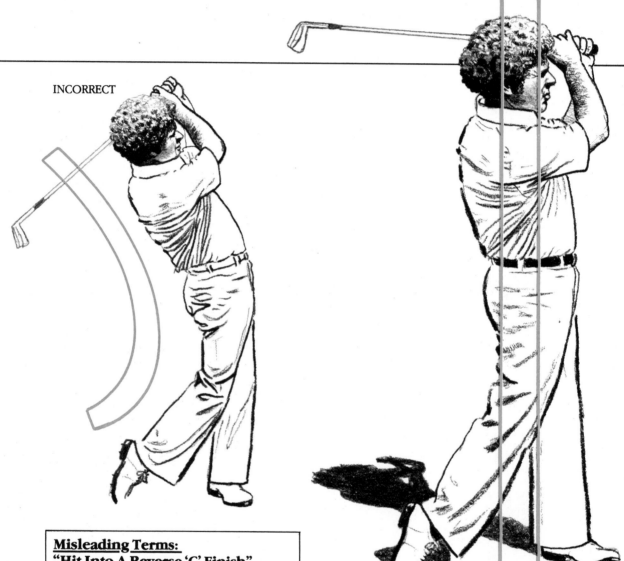

INCORRECT

Misleading Terms:
"Hit Into A Reverse 'C' Finish"

This misleading term is guaranteed to produce inconsistent shots, not to mention lower back problems. All the great strikers of the ball past and present finish the swing erect, with shoulders and hips level and facing the target.

player finishes in the inverted "C", that is, stays behind the ball, the arms are swinging the club while the body falls back or away. The golfer wants the arms and body to coordinate and go toward the target, which carries the player to the proper straight balanced finish.

All of this ties directly to the most popular excuse in golf—"Oops! I looked up." If a player stays behind the ball and hits into the inverted "C", where will the head and eyes go? If during the swing the body stays back, the spine will raise the head and eyes, placing the low point of the arc behind the ball so that the club will be coming *up* at impact causing the player to strike the upper half of the ball—topping it. In fact, a player could keep his head down, stay back, and conceivably experience the sheer horror of watching himself top the ball all day. A golfer must strike the ball a descending blow, down and through, and this can't be done with regularity if the body hangs back.

Consistently squaring the face of the club to the back of the ball at impact can be accomplished only by allowing the body to go with the arms and hands in the same natural manner employed to throw the shag bag through the door. As we shall see, when the golfer finishes properly, there should be the feeling of some pressure in the legs, but the erect level finish insures the total absence of pressure in the lower back.

Terms and phrases which enter the golfing language and attempt to shed light on the rapidly moving realities of the swing must be carefully scrutinized before a player adopts one as a swing key. Around the turn of the century, Harry Vardon wrote of "leading the downswing with the clubhead," "throwing the club to the right and a little behind the body," and starting the swing with

Swinging On the Level

Even the best players in the world consciously or unconsciously succumb to the siren song of golf's misleading terms. When Johnny Miller experienced his first prolonged wave of success on tour a few years ago, he was finishing his swing in the erect and balanced position characteristic of all the great strikers of the ball (left). Then he began noticeably bowing on the follow-through (right), and he went into a slump. This bow was caused by a reverse pivot. More recently Miller appears to have restored the proper "levels" to his swing and has begun to play winning golf again.

"only the arms moving until half way down." But as early sequence photos clearly indicated, Vardon didn't actually incorporate any of the moves he suggested.

Hogan was once quoted as asking with a note of disgust, "Coming off the ball—what the hell does that mean!" And how many times have I seen a man and a boy on the practice tee, and the man says, "Son, I can't play that well, but I know! Now, keep your head *down,* swing your left shoulder *under* and *slide* your hips!"

Remember, language at best can be subtly deceptive and "feel senses," as the Vardon example shows, can be absolutely treacherous. There's a simple test for a golfing term:

1) It must be easy to understand—not in the least abstract.

2) It must make good common sense.

3) It must not violate the rule of "cause and effect"···... (that is, it can't ask you to consciously do something when the club is traveling at approximately 100 mph which creates a physical impossibility).

4) It must be clearly visible in the swings of all of the great ball strikers.

CHAPTER THREE

THE BRACED CONNECTED ADDRESS

To introduce you to the concept of connection, I'd like to use an analogy to make your entire body sensitive to the proper feelings. From this general exercise, we will then discuss how a player learns to build the connections that culminate in the properly braced, connected address.

THE WEIGHTLIFTER'S POSITION

Suppose I were on a platform, holding a large golf bag of substantial weight, and you were standing below on the ground facing me. I indicate that I'm going to drop the bag to you and say, "Get ready!" How would you prepare to receive the weight?

Surely, without giving it a second's thought, you'd instinctively spread your feet to approximately shoulder width and brace yourself. You do this because your brain sends a message to your body: " 'Tie in' all of the large muscles to prevent possible physical danger!"

If I then asked you, just prior to passing the bag, to be kinesthetically aware of your bodily sensations, from the ground up, what would you feel?

Your feet would be gripping the ground, with the weight on the insides, running from the ball to the heel of each foot. Your legs would be automatically braced, your knees flexed slightly inward, and you would feel the large muscles on the inside of each leg tighten slightly, in readiness. The feeling would continue through the muscles of the posterior and on into the big muscles running up each side of the lower back.

You would also feel quite responsive in the larger muscles of the upper body, particularly in the large muscles of the upper back (the "lats") and the larger muscles in the chest area (the "pecs"). Notice that the upper arms naturally adhere to the sides of the chest area, bracing the upper torso. Also notice (and this surprises many people) that the most quiet or passive members of the entire body, at this point, are the forearms and the hands.

Shift your attention momentarily to your overall posture—legs braced, knees slightly flexed, hind quarters extended out a couple of inches beyond the backs of your heels, and the entire upper body (spine) held erect. Knees, hips and shoulders level, the head centered and up, the body perfectly balanced and poised.

We have created a situation where the hands and arms will receive the weight and be responsible for controlling it, but the task cannot be completed successfully without the natural integrated utilization of the larger muscles of the body. Thus, we have connection.

Suppose you tried to receive the weights leaning forward, with arms disconnected from the body, the center of the chest down, and the weight toward the toes? Several things could happen, all bad. Unquestionably, you would place undue strain on your back, probably causing you to either drop the bag or pitch forward off balance in your attempt to control it. Also, if you straightened your legs, rolled your posterior under and curved or hunched your spine, the force of the weight could again strain your back and force you to pitch backwards on your heels.

To reproduce the position and feelings exemplified by the weightlifter's position, grip a club as if it were a set of weights, and have a partner place his or her hands to either side of your own and press downward. Or you can create the same sensations alone by pretending to pick up the end of a heavy object like a desk or dining room table. As soon as you begin the process,

---

**COMMON DENOMINATOR #1
The golfer must create connection at the outset through a braced connected address position.**

To prepare to receive a heavy burden such as a golf bag full of clubs, you would not stand ramrod straight and extend your arms from the shoulder joints; if you did, you would drop the weight or fall off balance.

If, however, you set your feet apart, flexed and braced your legs and kept your extended arms connected to the large muscles in your torso, you would have no trouble receiving the weight.

Similarly, great strikers of the ball such as Gene Littler set up in a lithe, athletic manner, with all their large muscles tied in to body center, ready to support the dynamic task of executing the full golf swing.

NOTE: All likenesses of the great ball strikers used in this book are drawn precisely from actual photographs, with all details of swing mechanics and positioning rendered without modification of any kind.

INCORRECT

Gene Littler

COMMON DENOMINATOR I

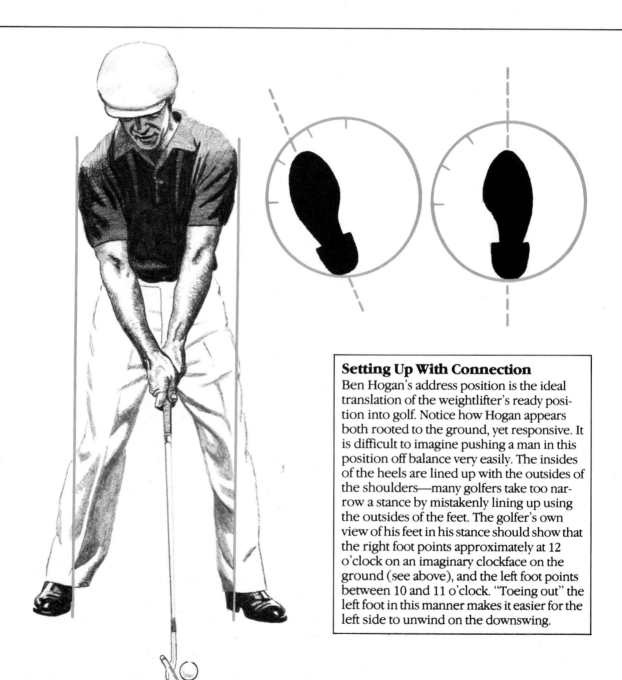

Setting Up With Connection

Ben Hogan's address position is the ideal translation of the weightlifter's ready position into golf. Notice how Hogan appears both rooted to the ground, yet responsive. It is difficult to imagine pushing a man in this position off balance very easily. The insides of the heels are lined up with the outsides of the shoulders—many golfers take too narrow a stance by mistakenly lining up using the outsides of the feet. The golfer's own view of his feet in his stance should show that the right foot points approximately at 12 o'clock on an imaginary clockface on the ground (see above), and the left foot points between 10 and 11 o'clock. "Toeing out" the left foot in this manner makes it easier for the left side to unwind on the downswing.

you will be able to experience all of the large muscles of the body "tying in." After doing this a few times, you should know whether or not you create any of these sensations in your own address position.

Among the pros I've worked with, Jim Colbert told me that the weightlifter's analogy held particular significance for him in that it provided a complete image of the correct address position, one which easily transferred to the set-up. (Colbert assumes, in my opinion, as good a position at the ball as any player on the tour, incidentally, so if you have the chance to watch him play, it wouldn't hurt to pay careful attention to, and even emulate, his address position.) By using the weights analogy, we have magnified or exaggerated the feelings of connection somewhat. But they should still be there when the golfer addresses the ball, even though the golf club only weighs a pound or less.

All good golfers set to the ball in a way that appears athletic. They're springy in the legs and body and soft and supple in the arms. Also, they position their feet so that the right foot is square to the intended line and the left foot is turned out slightly.

Correctly positioning the feet is another one of those relatively simple considerations that a multitude of golfers disregard. Let me give a surefire method for setting the feet properly, and then follow it with a short explanation as to why it is so important. Suppose I asked you to address a shot, setting your feet on two clocks that had been cemented to the ground? All you'd have to do, as you looked down, would be to place your right toe on 12 o'clock and your left toe between ten and 11 o'clock. If you boxed both feet, that is, placed both toes at 12 o'clock, you might be able to coil back reasonably well, but the boxed left foot would prevent the left side from unwinding properly on the downswing. If, on the other hand, you placed the right foot on, say, two o'clock and adopted a sort of duck walk stance, when you coil on the backswing you'll be forced to move weight to the outside of the right leg and foot. From there, you have no chance of moving the weight correctly to the left side. Good golf shots spring from the ground up, and unless the feet are placed as described, your swing dies in your shoes.

Another simple rule of positioning that is often violated by the average golfer has to do with the width of the stance. Perhaps 80 per cent of all golfers play from a stance that is too narrow. In bracing the legs properly, we are not only looking for good posture and balance, but also the creation of potential power. Braced means that when we coil into the backswing we can "charge" the right leg with energy, so that it is able to kick and recoil from the inside of the right foot on the downswing. As in the weightlifting analogy, we want the feet gripping the ground, the knees opposing, and a feeling of pressure on the insides of the thighs. When we are braced properly, we should be able to pump the legs back and forward as if they were pistons.

The majority of my students need a wider foundation in order to get their legs to work strongly. The general rule is: shoulder width for a full 5-iron, widening marginally with the longer clubs, and narrowing from the 6-iron to the wedges. However, many students misconstrue shoulder width, which should be measured from the tips of the shoulders to the *inside* of the heels, *not* from the tips of the shoulders to the outsides of the feet.

Proper position and posture create balance at the outset. If you think that you are braced correctly but have the feeling that your balance might be a little precarious, try this. Simply curl your toes upward inside your golf shoes. This will place the weight on the balls and the insides of the feet. It should immediately give you the sensation of added stability in your stance.

A lot of players address the ball in a kind of bow- or spraddle-legged stance with their weight carelessly distributed on the outsides of the feet. They look like retired rodeo riders. As pro Joe Porter told me one day as he looked across the practice tee, "That guy's legs look like two out-of-bounds stakes...one right...one left!" To show you how damaging this posture can be, and why I repeat and insist on the necessity of bracing the legs, roll on to the outsides of your feet and try to jump. You can't get two inches off the ground!

By applying the ideas and feelings of the weightlifter's analogy to the proper address position, you will adopt a stance in which you create what I call the correct "levels." In other words, in the braced, connected address position you want a feeling that the knees, hips and shoulders are as level as possible. Knees and hips should be *exactly* level, and the right shoulder should be only slightly under the left because the right-hand grip is below the left on the club. When you assume the connected address and incline the entire spine forward to measure to the ball, you create your levels. The proper angle of the spine and the shoulder plane of the swing are now in place. After this, the key is to maintain your levels throughout the swing.

In teaching individuals who have a tendency to dip going back or through, I treat the center of the chest— that area at or just below the sternum—as a level, also. I tell them that "center" moves in an arc back and slightly up, down through, and back up during the course of the swing. This is so because at address the upper torso is essentially an inclined cylinder coiling back and through. Helping the player to feel that center moves level prevents dipping and the resultant disconnection.

Curtis Strange keys on the idea of maintaining his levels. He never has the feeling that the left shoulder goes down on the backswing or that the right shoulder goes down, or under, on the downswing. A player should feel that he or she simply coils or uncoils on the planes or levels naturally created in the set-up.

Tom Watson keys on maintaining the same inclination of the spine from address to finish. Watson feels that applying what I term the concept of maintaining levels to his spinal column is a personal key which promotes consistency.

Hogan once suggested that relaxation over the ball was not really possible. You want comfort and balance but there must be what he called "live tension," too. I think that describes the feeling well. But, as we move into the elements of the braced connected address position, let me warn you against over-bracing. Remember, the idea is to create athletic responsiveness. We want live connected relationships, not muscular restriction or rigidity.

BUILDING A BRACED CONNECTED ADDRESS

In building connection, we must proceed sequentially from the grip, to the body, to the ground. Initially, we'll focus on the grip, which is the connecting link in the golf swing. In learning to grip the club properly, we begin the process of connecting the arms to the body. Once this is accomplished, and the upper body is positioned correctly, it's a simple matter to brace the legs

---

Grip —"Clap" The Hands On Square

In terms of connection, the most important aspect of the grip, regardless of whether you use the Vardon, the interlock or the ten-finger style, has to do with the position of the hands relative to each other and the target. They should always be placed on the club as though in a clapping position, with palms facing each other and with the back of the left hand and the palm of the right hand square to the target line.

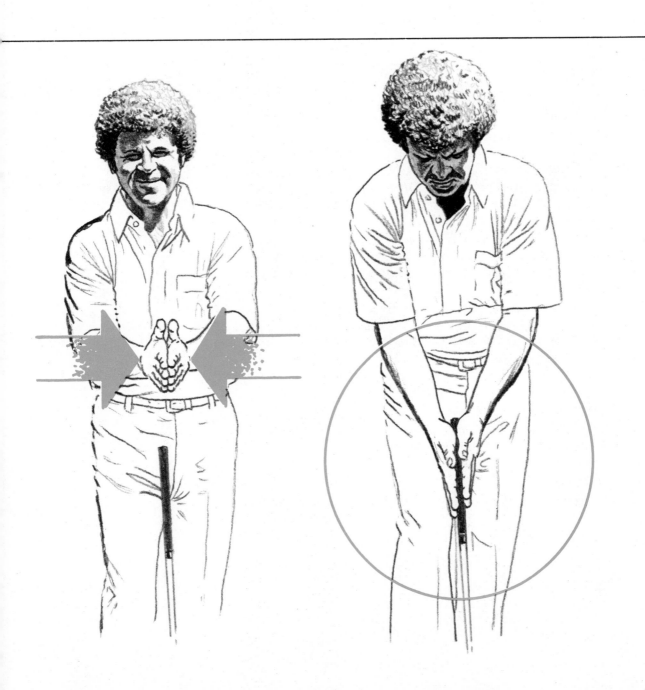

and, in essence, set the entire anatomy upon Mother Earth in a balanced connected fashion.

The Grip

Over the years, countless instructional articles and the early chapters of instructional golf books have dealt with the grip and address position by likening the process to the building of a proper foundation, and although the analogy is accurate, somewhere along the way 90 per cent of the golfing public evidently lost interest. For in spite of the fact that millions of golfers have read thousands of pages stressing the absolute necessity of a correct grip and set-up, most still stand to the ball like they're suffering from stomach cramps, and employ a grip more aptly suited to starting a heavy-duty lawn mower.

This is a constant thorn in the side of a serious teacher. Hitting the damn thing, consistently, is the hard part. Gripping the club and setting up to the ball reasonably well can't be as difficult as most average players make it. It wouldn't be logical to expect a recreational golfer to swing the club like a tour star, but there shouldn't be any reason why an intelligent weekender can't grip the club, and stand to the ball in much the same manner as a touring professional.

Obviously, the problem is not one of intelligence, but of patience—or more properly—impatience. The considerations of grip and address are necessary evils.

First, let me make some general observations about the grip, and then we will discuss its function as the connecting link.

There are three basic ways of gripping the club—the Vardon or overlapping grip, the interlocking grip, and the ten-finger grip. As to the type a player employs, I'm not particular. Ben Hogan and Byron Nelson, who in my opinion are the premier ball strikers in the history of the game, both used the Vardon or overlapping grip. Jack Nicklaus, undoubtedly the greatest player the game has yet produced, has won everything employing an interlocking grip, and Art Wall, whose long and successful tournament career has been highlighted by the fact that he holds the record for holes-in-one, accomplished all this with a ten-finger grip.

So, exceptional golf can be played with any of the three grips, and a player should not be persuaded to change to one grip if another feels more comfortable.

The most important aspect of the grip, regardless of type, has to do with the position of the hands relative to each other and the target. They must be square or in a "clapping" position, and that relationship must be maintained as you place the hands and wrap the fingers around the club. The palms must be facing each other, with the back of the left hand and the palm of the right hand perpendicular to the target line.

The Left Hand

With the left hand square to an imaginary target, place the club in the hand so that it runs diagonally across the palm at the angle it would assume at address. (1) Place the club underneath the pad at the rear of the hand and curve your index finger around the shaft. (2) Now, lift the club directly up in front of your left side, being sure you don't reach across the body, toward the right, but straight out so that the left elbow points to the left hip bone. Take the club to waist height. As you do this, you will notice that the pec and lat muscles in your back and chest have responded by tightening slightly. There should be the distinct sensation that you have done more than simply pick up the club with your hand and arm. At this moment, arm and shoulder are beginning the natural process of connecting to the body.

Suppose I adopted the braced, connected address position and assumed the heel pad and index finger grip just explained. I then ask you to pull steadily on the shaft in an attempt to wrest the club from my hand or pull me off balance. From this grip, you could jerk it from my hand . . . but as long as you pull, a resisting force is being created through the pecs and lats and the center of the chest—my entire upper body mass. Presuming that you and I are nearly the same weight, I can resist your attempt to take the club from my hand or pull me off balance no matter how hard you exert.

However, if I squeeze tightly with the last three fingers of the left hand, you can pull me—without jerking the club—rather easily to my toes. This is because in the second example I have created tension rather than connection. The tightening of the last three fingers tightens the left forearm from the elbow down. I am now no longer counterbalancing the force of your pulling with the connected body but simply with a tension-ridden arm and hand. In essence, I have broken off my counterbalancing force. This is another example that should give you a feeling of how arm tension breaks connection, and forces the arms and body to operate in opposition to one another—an independence that will destroy any opportunity to make a decent swing.

If experience is the best teacher, these two exercises should settle any lingering questions you have as to proper grip pressure. The grip pressure in the left hand is not in the last three fingers as is often taught. You should never squeeze the club. Simply let the club lie there comfortably, wrapping the fingers lightly around

Connection In The Grip — Left Hand
Hold the club lightly in the left hand, exerting pressure only with the first finger, not the last three fingers as is often recommended. The latter suggestion promotes disconnection by creating tension in the left forearm. Someone pulling on the club could yank you off balance because the only force you would be resisting with was coming from your forearm and shoulder joint or socket, not from the body. If, however, you grasp the club under the heel pad, with index finger simply wrapped around the handle, your arm would remain tied into your large back and shoulder muscles, which you could then use to resist the outsider's pulling force.

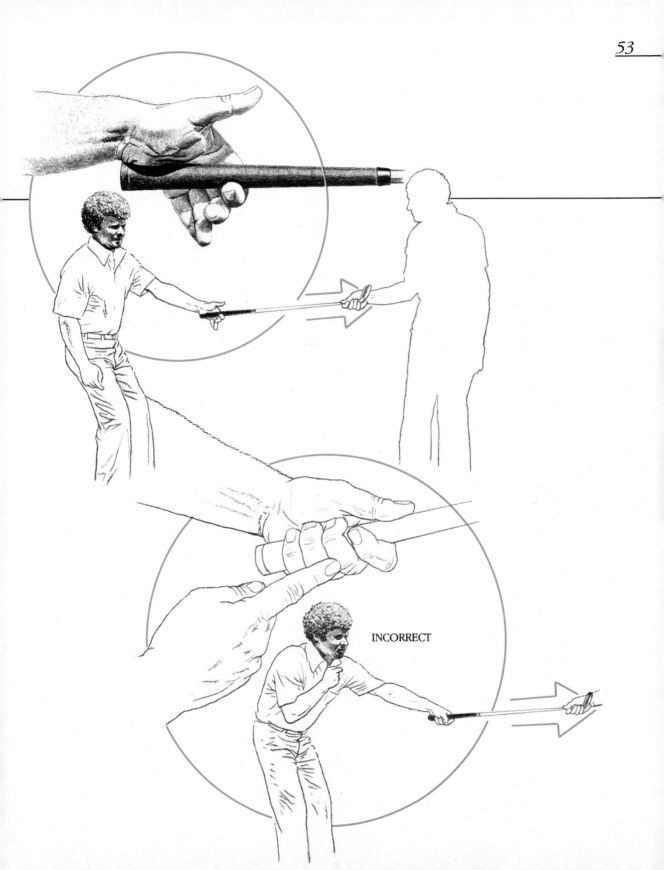

INCORRECT

it. With the relationship between the heel pad and index finger intact, the club in essence creates its own force.

Walter Hagen said it well years ago when he suggested that you exert no more pressure on the grip of a golf club than you would on a fountain pen. Also, if we strangle the club at address, using most of our gripping strength, what happens when the club is traveling approximately 100 mph in the impact area? The club *must* loosen in the hands because we don't possess the added strength to control it! With the light grip, the hands react naturally to the centrifugal force of the swing and create the proper grip pressure needed to control the club throughout.

The Right Hand

With the left hand properly on the club and held waist-high in front of the left side, and the right hand facing the target, slip the middle and ring fingers around the shaft, insuring that the grip of the club is against and underneath the base pads of the fingers, and that the club is resting in the fingers.

The right-hand grip is always "up" on the club. Never let the right hand slip "under" the shaft so that the grip is partially in the palm. Also, never exert grip pressure with the thumb or forefinger of the right hand. You can experience what this will do by grasping your right forearm with your left hand, and squeezing your right thumb and index finger together. Notice the tenseness in the muscles of the right forearm.

In the grips of the great ball strikers I have seen slight variations in the position of the left hand. A few place it on the club in what is called the stronger position, that is, the back of the left hand may face a few degrees right of the target line. However, the right hand is always up

Connection In The Grip — Right Hand
With the left hand properly on the club and held about waist high and the right hand facing the target (upper left), slip the middle and ring fingers of the right hand around the shaft, insuring that the grip of the club is against and underneath the base pads of the fingers, and that the club is resting in the fingers. Don't let the right hand slip under the shaft so that the grip is partially in the palm. Large view shows assembled grip.

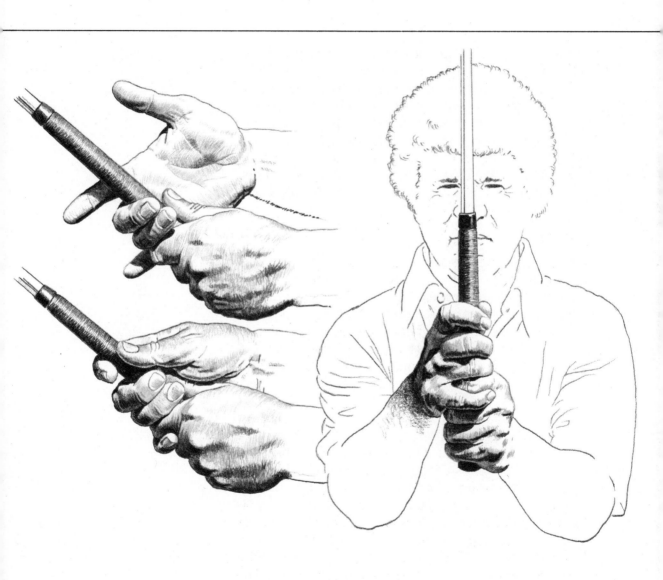

on the club, never under the shaft, and the grip is always in the middle two fingers as mentioned.

I believe that the terms strong and weak, relative to the grip, can be misleading. They have become synonymous with hooking and slicing the ball, strong being referred to as the hook grip and weak as a slice grip. This has led teachers over the years to advocate changing the position of the hands to produce certain types of shots. We shall see later that this is doing it the hard and inconsistent way. The strongest grip in golf is the one we've been discussing, with the hands absolutely square or in the clapping position on the club.

Also, many teachers and players place great emphasis on how many knuckles are showing, or where V's are pointing. This is really meaningless because the number of knuckles a player can see depends upon the position of the hands relative to where the player sets them at address. You can prove this to yourself very simply.

Grip the club as you normally do, and pretend for a moment you are lanky Don January. That is, stand erect with your hands up and your left wrist arched. Now look down, and you probably can see only one knuckle—if any. Without changing your grip, change characters. Pretend you are the shorter Hubert Green. Thus you would bend over, shoving your hands considerably closer to the ground. Now look down, and you can probably see all four knuckles and the V's may be pointing toward the beer stand! Although these two players position themselves to the ball differently, both have fine grips and so will you, if you place your hands on the club as suggested and remember not to get confused by metacarpals and imaginary letters.

Finally, gripping the club properly reduces to two things—hand position on the club and grip pressure. If there is something faulty about your grip, checking these two will uncover the problem immediately.

Connecting The Arms To The Body

In learning to grip the club correctly, the left hand heel pad and index finger exercise introduced you to an awareness of the fact that gripping the club involves more than wrapping the hands around the shaft. We noticed that there was a natural tendency for the left arm to seek connection with the left shoulder. In lesson situations, I'll often ask a golfer to point to his or her shoulder. Usually, the player will point toward the top of the shoulder, approximately where the shirt stops and the sleeve begins—designating the shoulder *joint*. This is understandable as in our daily lives we see our shoulder as something that helps us reach away from the body, to pick up coffee cups and telephones, take clothing off of hangers, or change light bulbs. However, if we use the shoulder joints in this manner while swinging a golf club, we'll end up wishing we had stayed at the office or attended to some household chores. We never want to swing a golf club from the shoulder joints.

From this point on, when we mention the shoulder, understand that we are referring to the shoulder area. Your golfing shoulders include the upper arms and the 'lats' and 'pecs,' the large back and chest muscles. The golfer must first connect the left arm to the shoulder area. We are teaching this because in the swings of all the great ball strikers, the shoulders swing the arms. The arms never move independently, operating from the shoulder joints. Many fine players may feel that the arms pull the shoulders or express various individual feelings. However, a look at their swings indicates what really happens. They operate as a unit. To give you a

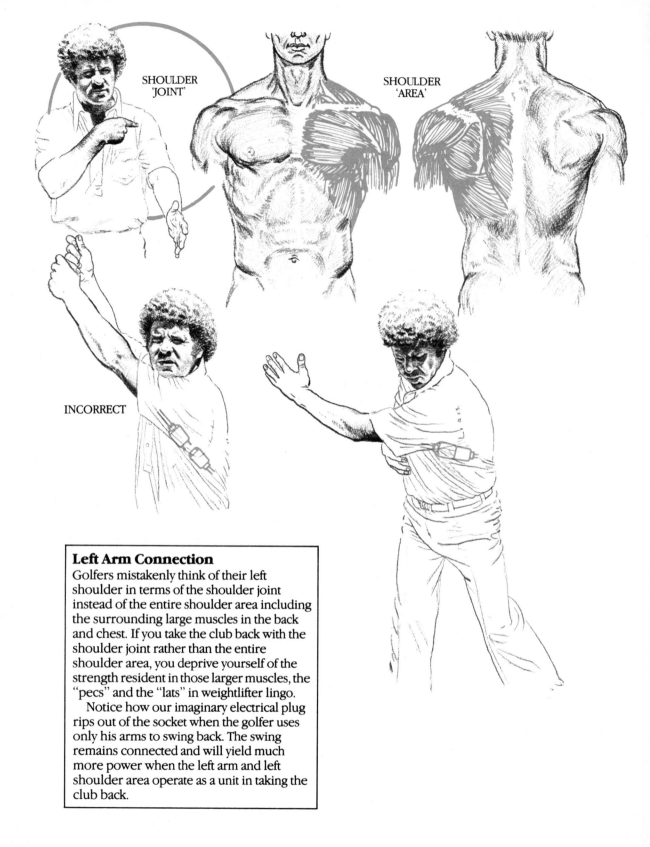

SHOULDER 'JOINT'

SHOULDER 'AREA'

INCORRECT

Left Arm Connection

Golfers mistakenly think of their left shoulder in terms of the shoulder joint instead of the entire shoulder area including the surrounding large muscles in the back and chest. If you take the club back with the shoulder joint rather than the entire shoulder area, you deprive yourself of the strength resident in those larger muscles, the "pecs" and the "lats" in weightlifter lingo.

Notice how our imaginary electrical plug rips out of the socket when the golfer uses only his arms to swing back. The swing remains connected and will yield much more power when the left arm and left shoulder area operate as a unit in taking the club back.

INCORRECT

Ben Hogan

...And "Disconnection"

In his earlier years, Ben Hogan had an over-swing and got into a lot of difficulty hooking the ball. As the smaller sketch shows, what really happened on his backswing was that he pulled his arms across the chest and then picked the club up, lifting from the shoulder joint.

In the remodeled swing with which he became dominant in golf in his time, the left arm remained connected throughout the backswing, as evident in the larger figure. Here he is coiled in a hitting position that not only will draw power but great consistency from the use of his body's major muscle groups.

visual appreciation of this, study the swing sequence of any great player (as in Chapter Ten), directing your attention to the shoulder area. You will notice that the connection created at address is maintained throughout the swing. The upper portion of the left arm never separates from the left side until late in the follow-through.

I've found that a good way to get this idea across to players is to use the analogy of a standard two-prong household plug and wall socket. At address, when the left arm comes straight out from the side—as if you were shaking hands lefthanded—you can feel the upper portion of the bicep and the pec muscle touching a fraction beneath the upper arm. Suppose you had two prongs in the side of the chest, and you plugged the two together? This doesn't mean to contract the muscles of the bicep or pec. Don't ram the plug into the wall; simply complete the contact so the two are touching. Now you have connected the left arm to the body. And this next statement is of paramount importance: wherever it starts, it never changes. (It will unplug naturally, late in the followthrough. If it didn't, you'd screw yourself into the ground.)

Another way to get a feel for this is to hit some medium or short irons with a handkerchief under your left shoulder. If you drop the handkerchief, you've unplugged, or disconnected, allowing the arms to work independently of the body.

The connected left arm creates the consistent radius of the golf swing. You never want to allow the left arm to get "longer" or "shorter" from the point of connection. One of the most common faults in the golf swing takes place here, and I refer to it as "run-off." When a player swings the club from the shoulder joints, working the arms independently and unplugging his connection, the arms get longer but the body has not gone with them. The result is longer arms and a shorter swing arc. Since the arms have "grown" on the backswing, they will have to be pulled or sucked back in on the downswing if the player is going to make contact with the back of the ball. There is no chance of doing this consistently.

With the legs braced, spine erect, and the left shoulder connected, arm run-off can be prevented when the player measures to the ball. Measuring creates the uniform radius of the swing at the outset, and maintaining connection preserves it. A player should place the club behind the ball by employing a semi-sitting position, by lowering the body without changing body posture. Thus, the low point of the arc is established with connection. In this regard, Hogan's analogy of a golfer lowering as if to sit on a spectator sports stick was excellent.

The most common error at this stage is a player beginning the process of connecting, only to destroy it by bending the spine, which drops the chest forward and down, threatening balance and erasing the proper levels at address. If the back is humped over, center is dropped down and the player can only begin the swing from the shoulder joints. Also, when center is down, the butt of the club is out of plane immediately and the backswing can't begin without hand-arm manipulation.

Some readers may have noticed that a number of exceptional players don't sole the club on the ground behind the ball at address. Nicklaus and Green come immediately to mind. I don't advocate that all golfers adopt this when they play. Some have, only to discover that in the second round of the third flight of the club

INCORRECT

Measuring To The Ball
Once the legs are braced, the spine is erect or nearly erect (there may be a slight tilt) and the left arm is properly connected to the left shoulder area, the golfer maintains connection by measuring to the ball—placing his club behind the ball by employing a semi-sitting position and thus creating a radius for the swing that should not change. In the sequence showing Tom Watson's swing, imagine that the line between the center of his chest and the butt of his club is a taut string. When a golfer has properly measured to the ball, this distance never varies. The string does not snap or become slack at any stage; the movement of the club never becomes independent of the movement of the body.

championship, their nerves weren't sound enough to keep the club still. But, at home or while practicing, measuring to the ball without grounding the club will give you an excellent awareness of the feeling of a connected address and a more precise appreciation of the radius of the swing.

When a player measures to the bottom of the ball on an iron shot (lightly soling the club to the ground) he has created the connected relationships necessary to deliver a crisp descending blow down and through in the impact area.

When the ball is set up, on a tee, measuring to the bottom of the ball insures that the player will contact the ball at the bottom of the arc where the club is traveling level. In this way, the 12° loft of your driver face will provide the correct shot shape—that is, the desired combination of length, accuracy and trajectory.

When a player measures with connection, he extends the club from the lat muscle because he coils the hands, arms, shoulders and body away together. Swinging from the shoulder joints creates an immediate disconnection in that you are not using either your newly defined golfing shoulder and thus your body. You'll often hear a player observe that another player's swing is "all arms." The player has swung the club from the shoulder joints. Usually, severe run-off is created by the golfer trying to attain what he mistakenly perceives to be greater extension. But by disconnecting—making the arms longer, he has actually shortened his arc.

Once you've placed the left hand on the club and connected the left arm to the shoulder area, swing your right arm by the right hip pocket as if you were going to shake hands with the club. Once you set your right hand grip as explained previously, the right arm and shoulder

Right Arm Connection

The most natural position of the right arm at the top of the backswing—akin to a throwing motion—is also the most effective because it permits the arm to work in tandem with the large muscles in the right shoulder area. Keeping the elbow tucked into the ribcage, or lifting it unnaturally high, as shown, are forms of disconnection because effective contact with the right shoulder area is lost. Some golfers, such as Miller Barber, depicted here, naturally set the right arm in a higher position at address. Notice, though, that Barber's arm never changes in relation to the chest and 'lat' area of the right side. Arm and shoulder area move back as a unit and as he continues to coil, his left knee goes back and up with his arm. Barber does not have a 'flying right elbow' because he created connection at address and maintained it throughout.

INCORRECT

INCORRECT

Miller Barber

are in a natural position, and from here with both arms connected, the arms and shoulders go away together.

As to connecting the right arm, we come to another area replete with instructional contradiction. A lot of players and teachers have advocated that golfers keep the right arm and elbow down and in toward the body at address, and against the right side of the backswing.

All of this comes from a phobia about a flying right elbow. The right elbow has to come away from the side when the player moves into the strong backswing position. Anything else is unnatural. The next time you go down to hit a bucket of balls, prove this to yourself with a simple exercise. Without the club, but with a golf ball held in your right hand, assume the braced, connected address position. Now throw the ball vigorously out onto the range. How did your right arm react to throwing the ball? If you tried to freeze your right elbow against your right side, you'd throw some kind of a wild blooper, and the feeling would be totally unnatural. So also, if you swept the right arm out away from your body, so that the elbow shot semi-skyward (this would be a genuine flying right elbow), the feeling and results would be equally as discomforting. However, if you threw the ball naturally, without giving it a second thought, your right arm motion would very nearly approximate the motion of the great ball strikers during the backswing.

Right arm and shoulder connection is really a matter of natural positioning and although the arm begins folding in the middle of the backswing the idea is, like the left arm and shoulder, to have the right lat, pec and shoulder operate as a unit. We don't want the right arm operating from the shoulder joint, independently of the right side of the upper body.

Once in a while, after discussing right arm connection, a student will ask, "Doesn't Jack Nicklaus or Miller Barber disconnect on the backswing?" The answer is no. Both players, particularly Barber, set the right arm in a higher position at address than their fellow professionals. Consequently the right arm comes away from the body a little quicker. But the hand, arm, pec, lat and shoulder all move as a unit and as the club passes waist high, there is an excellent illustration of total body connection. Nicklaus once said of the feelings in his backswing, "I swing back as if I were going to shake hands with my right hand . . . and then I reach for a cloud in the sky." But he reached with connection; he did not raise his arms from the shoulder joints, working them independently of the body. Neither does Barber.

There's a simple way to visualize this. Suppose a substantial rubber band were attached from Nicklaus' left elbow to his left knee. You would notice as he coils back that his left knee goes back and up with his arms. You would also notice that his left shoulder stays just as it started—plugged in. At the top, the right hand, arm and shoulder move into a strong position and the right elbow is pointing down. Nicklaus creates his connections at address and then maintains the connective relationships throughout, from the ground up.

COMMON DENOMINATOR The golfer must create connection at the outset through a braced connected address position.

CHAPTER FOUR

THE PRE-SWING ROUTINE

I f there is one rule in movement sport, it is that every accomplished athlete has a pre-set routine that he carries out, step by step, each time he prepares to execute an intended activity. Countless golfers destroy any chance of making a connected golf swing moments after they take the club they're planning to use from the bag. They approach the ball in a haphazard, jerky fashion, set the club behind it, and instantly turn to stone.

Virtually all the great players in golf have used a sequence involving basically five pre-swing moves to prepare for a standard shot. Players with sound, repeating pre-swing patterns also learn much faster, incidentally, so if you incorporate these same five steps into your own routine, and practice them until they become so automatic you never have to think of them, you'll be in a much better position to consistently set up and swing with connection.

STEP 1

Standing erect with hips and shoulders level, grip the club with the left hand by the side. Lift it to waist level, opposite your left side and with connection.

Exceptional players approach a golf shot with the right foot forward, closer to the ball, and the left foot next to it. The upper body is slightly open to the target. Ideally, eyes, shoulders, hips and knees are as level as possible. Preservation of these levels is your best insurance against alignment problems.

The club is gripped in the left hand first. The left arm rests comfortably against the left side, insuring connection. From this position, the left hand can be placed on the club most naturally, with the blade square and the back of the hand facing the target.

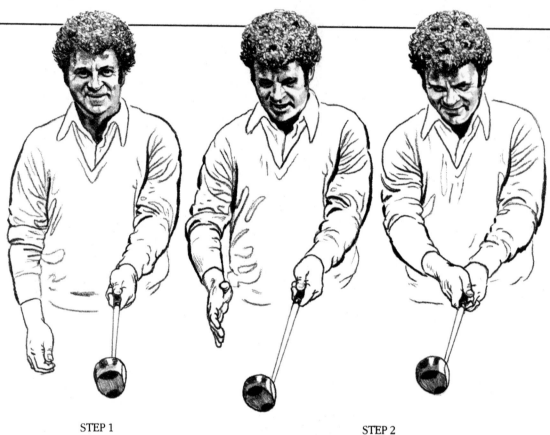

STEP 1   STEP 2

The Pre-Swing Routine

1. Standing erect with hips and shoulders level, grip the club with the left hand by the side. Lift it to waist level, opposite your left side with connection.

2. Place the right hand on the club, and "look" your grip on square.

3. Set the right foot, aim the blade and immediately return your eyes to the target.

4. Slip the left foot in by the right with the ball opposite the left heel.

5. Readjust the right foot to the final stance position while the head and eyes remain on the target.

STEP 3   STEP 4   STEP 5

The left hand is then lifted up and in front of the left side. The most common error here is to reach across the body—to the right—instead of straight out from the left side. Reaching across creates an immediate disconnection between arm and shoulder, and forces unwanted manipulation in order to square the back of the left hand with the leading edge of the blade. Remember, the left arm is on the side and the left elbow points down and in front of the body.

STEP 2

Place the right hand on the club, and 'look' your grip on square.

With the left hand in a shake-hands position, swing the right hand naturally up from the side to meet it. Be sure that the right hand goes on the club in the middle two fingers just below the fatty part of the callous pad. Now both arms are in front of your left side. Palms of hands oppose each other, in the clapping position, with the back of the left hand and the palm of the right hand both square to the target.

Avoid re-gripping the club as many golfers do while adjusting their feet and sighting the target. This habit invites disconnection by destroying the square relationship of the hands, blade and target. This way you minimize extraneous hand movement during the set-up and can move immediately into the job of alignment.

STEP 3

Set the right foot and aim the blade.

This begins the process of placing the feet in the correct position. The right foot should be placed approximately eight to ten inches behind the ball. This will prevent two common mistakes that cause disconnected alignment. If you walk to the ball and set the left foot first, you're looking across your target line at the outset and it is almost impossible to aim the blade properly. With the right foot in position first, you can aim the blade accurately.

The second common error made at this stage is to lean to the right and tilt the head as if you're sidewinding into the set-up. Here again, though, setting the eyes askew just makes proper alignment more difficult, so try to remain erect and level through knees, hips and shoulders as you set the club behind the ball and aim the blade.

Once the blade is properly aimed, return your attention to the target.

STEP 4

Slip the left foot in by the right with the ball opposite the left heel.

Having properly positioned the right foot and aimed the blade, you should slip the left foot to a point no more than 15 inches from the right.

Learn to do this automatically, without having to look at the feet in the process. Bear in mind that on all standard full shots the ball is played just off the inside of the left heel. Most golfers disconnect their address position by stepping too far forward with the left foot, which places the ball too far back in the stance. Since we have already aimed the blade in the previous step, we know where we're going, and consequently during this phase the head stays up with the eyes on the target.

STEP 5

Readjust the right foot to the final stance position while the head and eyes remain on the target.

This depends on the type of shot the player faces, in that a short iron requires a narrower stance than a full drive, but I will assume that you know that stance width varies relative to the club.

The most common cause of alignment problems crops up in this final phase of the set-up routine. Players try to adjust, or realign, while looking at their feet or the ball. In effect, they try to make the body go where they think the target is. But your eyes will adjust your body to the target accurately if you'll let them. Doing it the wrong way is analogous to a shortstop fielding a ground ball, then looking at his feet instead of at his first-baseman before throwing.

Once you've made the final adjustment of feet, and your eyes return from the target to the ball, it's time for the swing to begin.

An Option

If you can set the right foot and aim the blade with the upper body erect and slightly open, as described in Step 3, fine. However, many players at this stage hunch over, bending the spine forward and down, destroying their levels. With the center of the chest down, the arms will work from the joints or sockets destroying the 'lowered shoulders' we created earlier. So, if it feels more natural for you to place the feet together to retain erect and level posture, perform this step with feet together. Then, with head and eyes on the target, set the left foot, "feeling" the correct ball position off the left heel, and finally adjusting the right foot.

CHAPTER FIVE

TRIANGLE AND CENTER

The triangle and center are reference points to help you both understand and feel connection in its role as the moving constant in the golf swing.

When a golfer assumes the braced connected address position, the relationship between the shoulders, arms and hands forms a triangle, when viewed from straight on. During the swing, from waist high to waist high, back and through, this triangle remains clearly visible. As the club passes waist-high on the backswing, it may appear that the triangle breaks down. From a side view, however, it can be seen that as the club moves toward the top, the right arm and shoulder work up and back, with the right elbow pointing down and behind the golfer, but the right arm folds within the triangular shape. So also, at waist-high, on the follow-through, the left arm begins to fold on the body, but again, the triangular shape is maintained into the completed finish. Ideally, a player wants to stay with the triangle throughout the swing.

To experience the triangle-center feeling, try the following exercise. Take a driver, and grip down on the shaft until the butt of the club touches the middle of the chest about an inch up on the sternum. This point I call center. Keeping the butt of the club touching center, swing the triangle of arms, hands, and club back and through, waist-high to waist-high. Repeat this exercise several times being particularly aware of the feelings generated. It should become apparent that center coils in an arc back and slightly up, down through and back up. Also, center never stops moving throughout the course of the swing. Center represents the middle of the upper body mass. With repetition, you should have the sensation that you are swinging the triangle with center. This insures that the larger muscles of the legs and torso

INCORRECT

INCORRECT

Check Your "Triangle And Center"

In the swings of all the great strikers of the ball, the hands, arms and shoulders work as a unit throughout, and this unit works in a never-changing relationship to body center. An easy way to determine this at address is to check that the arms and shoulders form an isosceles triangle (two sides equal), as they do in the likeness of Hogan (whose address position is an exquisite model in all respects).

In the proper set up, a vertical line drawn from the butt of the club upward points to the sternum or left breast. Any deviation, as shown in the two small drawings, destroys the triangle. When the hands are pushed forward, the arms-shoulders triangle becomes irregular and the club no longer ties into body center. By creating an angle, instead of a triangle, at address, the golfer produces instant disconnection.

initially control the arms and hands—another way of introducing the feeling of connection into the swinging action.

Center is merely a point of reference and does not lead the swing. The swing should begin with a rhythmic kick of the left foot and left knee which immediately introduces the sequential coiling of the left side, the triangle and center. In other words, the backswing operates from the ground up, through center with connection. This interrelationship happens so rapidly that it is difficult for the untrained eye to appreciate the sequence. (It is perhaps most apparent in the syrupy backswing of Julius Boros.) So also, the downswing begins from the ground up with a kick of the right foot and right knee immediately followed by the sequential connected recoiling of the right side and center.

Center is always the reactor, never the initiator. If the golfer mistakenly tries to move behind the ball, through it, and past it with center only, the result will be a disconnected waving of the upper body back and through. A fixation on using center improperly destroys the leg brace and the coiling and recoiling activity which is the hallmark of the great ball strikers. The idea of swinging the triangle with center is a reference to provide an awareness of what the upper body actually does in a connected swing, in response, or as an immediate natural reaction to the coiling and recoiling of the legs.

At waist-high in the backswing, the connected coiling of the triangle causes the left knee to break in well behind the point where the ball would be addressed. You should be able to feel the large muscles on the insides of the legs, and as you conclude the abbreviated backswing, also notice that your weight is predominantly on the inside of the right foot.

Triangle-Center Drill

Choke down on your driver so that the butt of the club rests on your sternum, then swing back and through a number of times. This will help you experience the sensations connected with swinging in the good arms-shoulders triangle from body center throughout. Both at waist level on the backswing and at waist level on the follow-through, the toe of the club points straight in the air. In performing this drill—and in making the full swing—check to be sure that is the position of your club, for it ensures that at impact the club will be square.

As you swing through to the waist-high finish, keeping center and the triangle moving together, notice that your weight has shifted completely to your left side—you could pick your right foot off the ground. During the through swing, you should experience much the same feeling encountered when you threw the shag bag earlier. The point is, you can't swing the triangle with center correctly without incorporating the entire body from the ground up.

As to upper body sensations, notice that at waist-high on the backswing the right arm has moved away from the body and is just beginning to fold naturally. The left arm is not rigid or stiff, but comfortably extended from the lat muscle. If you held this position and had someone pull the club, moving it to the place where you would normally grip it, you would have maximum extension of the clubhead with connection.

What if you find that this exercise feels uncomfortable or restrictive, or both? In the first place, you've probably never tried to make an abbreviated swing with the butt of the club touching your chest, so it has to feel different. But, and this is more important, you have probably never taken the club away from the ball with your hands, arms, shoulders . . . and body, all working in concert.

You could generate a feeling more closely resembling that of your usual swinging action if you allowed the butt of the club to move away from center almost the instant you began swinging. Try it, leaving the butt of the club touching center as you start, but making no conscious effort to keep it there. Chances are the butt of the club will move off your chest before you move the clubhead a foot or more. Why? Because you took the club away from the ball predominantly with the hands, arms and shoulder joints. Center, i.e., your body, stayed at home.

You destroyed virtually every sensation created earlier when you did the exercise correctly.

Starting with the grip, you picked the club up, somewhat, with your hands, creating an angle off the tip of the triangle almost immediately. The arms moved independently. You'll notice you "bent the prongs," or completely unplugged the left arm from the shoulder. Your right arm, instead of moving naturally away from the body, broke inward and downward. At waist-high, you had a falsely extended left arm and thus shortened the arc of the clubhead. By failing to swing the triangle with center, you didn't feel the larger muscles of the legs or body react, and the left knee didn't break in properly behind the ball. By failing to move center you destroyed the connective relationships, all the way to the ground. Practically, by doing this, you've taken the larger muscles of the body out of the swing and consigned the entire task of striking to the arms and hands. So effectively, in a fraction of a second, you created an unwanted angle with the hands, disconnected both arms and the body.

If you are a student of the game, the term one-piece takeaway probably crossed your mind when you performed the exercise correctly. For years, players have had difficulty with this move because of the manner in which it was taught. "Take the hands, arms and shoulders away in one piece," was the usual instruction. The practical result was that the club was pushed back with the hands, arms and shoulder joints. At this point, the only way to raise the club up is to produce an abrupt and unnatural cocking of the wrists, and lift the arms across the chest, continuing to operate from the shoulder joints. It felt restrictive or dead because the move was not made with either center or connection. So even though the fanning open of the club, or the early set of the wrists

COMMON DENOMINATOR #2
The golfer must begin the swing by taking the triangle and center away together.

All the great strikers swing the club back at least to waist level and sometimes somewhat beyond with the arms-shoulders triangle intact and the club remaining tied into body center, as the Nicklaus likeness demonstrates. Note how the body center (see shirt buttons) has coiled with the triangle, ensuring that the big muscles of the torso stay in the act.

Undue small-muscle manipulation during the takeaway, as in trying to "preset" the wrist cock or to "roll the hands" allows not only the hands but the club to work independently of your body center. Note how in both incorrect moves above, the butt of the club now points way off center. A lot of hand manipulation will be required again on the downswing in order to square up the club, and that can't be done consistently by any golfer.

INCORRECT

Jack Nicklaus

"Toe In The Air Is Square"

A simple way to acquire the feeling for the connected backswing and follow-through, in terms of the "triangle and center," is to trace the course of the club-head during your swing. Presuming that square is where you started at address, at waist-high on the back-swing the toe of the club should be in the air with the leading edge perpendicular to the ground as seen in this sequence of Lee Trevino. At waist-high on the follow-through, the toe is again in the air and the leading edge is perpendicular to the ground.

was avoided, the body center didn't go with the hands and arms, and in an attempt to prevent one kind of disconnection, another was created.

The initial move in the golf swing can't be performed properly unless the player swings the triangle back *with* center.

Your next question might well be, "Now that I've got the triangle waist-high what do I do?" The answer is, you shouldn't *have* to do anything. At approximately waist-high, the folding of the right arm and the momentum of the club cause the natural hinging of the wrists. Years ago, one of the old touring pros was quoted, "You're in the locker room changing your shoes and you hear two guys discussing 'wrist action'... You don't have to look, you know they're amateurs!" I agree. There should never be any conscious effort to cock or uncock the wrists during the golf swing. If the club is gripped correctly, and the triangle is taken back with center while maintaining connection, the wrists will do their job perfectly without your mental assistance. Allow it to happen. The pick and roll has a definite place in basketball, but no place in golf.

Let's briefly look at what happens to the face of the club during the triangle-center exercise and during a swinging action. Presuming that square is where we started at address, at waist-high on the backswing the toe of the club is in the air with the leading edge perpendicular to the ground. At waist-high on the follow-through, the toe is again in the air and the leading edge is also perpendicular to the ground. At waist-high, both back and through, toe in the air is square.

If at waist-high on the backswing the toe is pointing behind you and the face skyward, the club has been opened. If, conversely, the toe is pointing in front of you, and the face is looking toward the ground, the club has been closed. In both instances, it means you've made an unnecessary manipulation of the hands, wrists and arms, and a compensating manipulation will have to be made on the downswing if the club is to be returned square to the ball at impact.

If we are to return the clubface square to the ball consistently, the best way to achieve this is with no conscious manipulation of the wrists, but with connection. Conceivably, there could be some confusion in this area when a golfer studies the pictures of several of the great ball strikers. For instance, Gary Player hinges or sets the wrists early in the backswing. In 1955, when Ben Hogan retired from active competition, he spoke of making a conscious manipulation of the left wrist during the backswing that made his game hook-proof. Snead advocated taking the club "to waist-high before the wrists began hinging," and Nicklaus has incorporated a late hinging of the wrists into his swing.

But this is like looking at the small differences in the throwing actions of four great baseball pitchers. To me, these are matters of style. I say this because in the swings of Player, Hogan, Snead and Nicklaus, the hands as a unit stay in the center of the chest well beyond waist-high on the backswing, and when the triangle reappears in the downswing, the hands remain in the center of the chest well past waist-high on the follow-through: all swing the triangle with center while maintaining connection.

The average golfer who pre-sets the wrists or hinges early disconnects. Pre-setting or hinging the wrists, or picking up the club allows not only the butt of the club but the hands, as a unit, to be worked independently of center. From here, there is never the proper coil behind the ball. The arc is shortened and the swing loses its connection. This is why I stress the butt of the club in the center of the chest. By keeping this in mind, along with the idea of the triangle, the golfer will have the best chance of minimizing the extraneous movement and thus avoid the connection-breakers during the swing.

COMMON DENOMINATOR 2 The golfer must begin the swing by taking the triangle and center away together.

CHAPTER SIX

THE BACKSWING-- COILING BEHIND THE BALL

H ardly a day goes by when I don't meet at least one student who complains of a lack of distance and admits to having spent many frustrating years of trying to make a better weight shift, or a more positive move through the ball.

Almost without exception, these golfers have spent all of their time and energy after the fact. They can't swing the club through the ball correctly because they didn't swing it back correctly. It's as simple as that. Only by making a sound backswing can the player create the position and leverage that will produce a sound golf shot. In this respect, we might say that a golfer is only as good as his backswing. If you can't learn to swing the club back properly, you have no chance of playing consistently well.

Although it is relatively simple to illustrate and explain the connected backswing, some players have difficulty trying to produce the necessary changes. For the most part, the reason lies in the vast difference between what the great ball strikers actually do when they swing the club back, and what most instructors teach in this critical area. Here again, there are a number of misconceptions that have been accepted as gospel by a large majority of players. Several are so familiar that golfers are hesitant to disregard them; but as long as they remain, they

INCORRECT

Triangle And Center At The Top

Though the right arm necessarily folds or bends on the backswing, the basic arms-shoulder triangle tied into body center remains evident in all the great strikers of the ball at this phase of the swing.

Holding the right arm artificially close to the ribcage on the backswing, or letting it fly unnaturally high, are common causes of disconnection at the top; in each instance the club no longer operates from center and so will have to be manipulated with weak hand action on the downswing.

Julius Boros

Sam Snead

INCORRECT

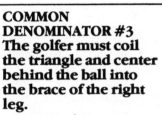

INCORRECT

COMMON DENOMINATOR #3
The golfer must coil the triangle and center behind the ball into the brace of the right leg.

Imagine a line rising straight up from the ball in the Watson likeness and you would see how he—as do all other great strikers of the ball—coils his body entirely behind the ball at the top of the backswing.

A good way to develop this all-important move in your own swing is to set up near a real or imaginary wall as shown and practice coiling back into it. Too much lateral movement: the golfer has swayed over the wall with his upper body. Not enough lateral movement: the golfer has tilted away from the wall into a reverse pivot—the curse of the vast majority of average golfers. With correct lateral movement: the brace of the right leg receives and holds the weight—the gun is loaded, ready to fire.

Tom Watson

represent mental and physical excess baggage that impedes any chance to approach one's real potential.

Almost to the word, the terminology generally applied to the teaching of the backswing fails to convey to students the essential elements that are readily observable in all of the backswings of the great ball strikers. As I mentioned earlier, I've found that the word "turn" does so much more harm than good that I have stopped using it entirely. The word "sway" is universally misunderstood. "Pivot" seems to mean more things to more people than the word democracy. Very few players have a clear understanding of what a reverse pivot is. Fewer yet can feel one!

While we are erasing the damage such words have done, we must also change our mind's image of the very shape of the backswing. In this regard, the video camera has been a godsend to me. There is no substitute for visual verification in teaching golf. Often, students will believe I am exaggerating their problem—until they see it, and compare it with correct positions. Sometimes, this moment of truth is coupled with minor hurt and temporary shock. (This, of course, means that a student has no clear conception at all as to what he or she is doing.) On a number of occasions, I've had students with excellent eyesight, three feet from a screen as big as some windows, witness their own backswing only to turn to me, seriously, and say, "Who was that?" I had a pretty good amateur once, who upon seeing his own backswing position compared to those of Snead and Nicklaus asked, "Do you have an airline sickness bag handy?"

It may prove a somewhat elusive task for you to compare the swing positions you achieve to those of the great players pictured in this book. Since you can't see

Reverse Pivot: Public Enemy No. 1
The notion of "turning" on the backswing has created more reverse pivots than the Arthur Murray Dance Studio. When weight tilts forward in the stance, as it must do if one simply turns or twists instead of coiling into the braced right leg, the swing is hopelessly underpowered. One must coil against the wall—but not sway—in order to store up energy for a dynamic downswing.

yourself swing you're going to have to concentrate on feeling your way into the correct positions. I originally considered suggesting that readers have their swings filmed or videotaped. But since I do this with my students, I know how difficult it is to do it correctly. Still toying with the idea, I decided to ask the opinions of a number of the touring pros I work with. The consensus was: a hospital patient wouldn't think of trying to film and interpret his own X-rays. The pros are right. So in this section, proceed slowly, taking the time to thoughtfully compare the swings of the greats with the illustrations which show common backswing errors.

THE MOVE BEHIND THE BALL

In looking at the fundamental elements of the backswing, I want to first deal with how a player should make the proper move behind the ball, and then deal with the misunderstandings that prevent players from achieving the position.

On any standard full shot, where the ball is played approximately off the left heel, all of the great ball strikers have coiled totally behind the ball at the top of the backswing. By this I mean that if we draw a vertical line through the center of the ball, at a right angle to the ground, and extend it six feet in the air, at the completion of the backswing all of the great strikers are totally behind that line.

How did they achieve this position? From a braced, connected address, they have taken the triangle with center and coiled the entire left side (the left foot, left knee, left hip and left shoulder, in a chain reaction—a straight line) into the "brace" or "set" of the right leg.

A player could feel this in reverse (left shoulder, left hip, left knee, left foot), or, as I've had players tell me,

Permissible Motion In The Backswing

Ben Crenshaw comes as close to moving "over the wall" as anyone in the top ranks on the tour today. Yet most ordinary golfers would be better off copying his move away from the ball than focusing on the much more limiting admonitions of "head still," "turn," "don't sway," etc. Joe Louis never knocked an opponent out by leaning his body *toward* the opponent's chin just prior to delivering the punch.

they may feel as if they take the right shoulder and pull the left side into the right side; or they may feel the left lat moving level to a position behind the ball as they swing toward the top. How an individual golfer feels the move is not important, provided he has moved to a place behind the ball in a strong connected position so he can recoil and hit it with authority. I often refer to this move as "loading the gun." As we shall see shortly, most average players try to play with an unloaded gun or end up with something that continually misfires.

Most of the mistakes players make on the backswing immediately or ultimately result in a reverse pivot, golf's unforgivable sin. Why do so many golfers commit the sin? The idea of turning is one reason. If a player thinks in terms of a turn, he or she will stop center from coiling laterally back, and level, as it should, or worse yet, move it down and forward. Why? Once players assume the braced connected address position, they are working from both hip joints. If you were to stand on one foot, like a flamingo, you could turn on the ball and socket of one joint until you lost your balance. But once you've braced the legs, at about shoulder width, and you're working from the insides of the legs, if you then try to turn, you will succeed only in turning against the left hip joint. This is really no more than a twist. Many teachers have stressed turning—"but with enough lateral movement to insure that the weight transfers to the right foot on the backswing"—or words to that effect. But this is vague. How much is enough? And as a practical matter, if the player concentrates on keeping the head still and turning, even if he's trying to introduce enough lateral movement to get weight to the right side, it almost never happens.

Let me now create a clear conceptual understanding

Subscribe to GOLF DIGEST now and SAVE 50%

Jack Nicklaus, Golf Digest's Chief Playing Editor, brings you his personal instruction series in every issue. Follow along with Jack as he shows you the mechanics and strategies he uses in his own game.

Improve your game with lessons from Tom Watson, Hal Sutton and other top touring pros who write exclusively for Golf Digest.

Bob Toski and the rest of the teaching professionals of the Golf Digest Schools will coach you in all aspects of the game.

You'll get all of the best step-by-step instruction as well as tournament news, reports on equipment, golf resorts and much more. Just fill out the coupon below and mail it today!

LOWEST PRICE AVAILABLE ANYWHERE!

of what a coil is. Suppose you took your address position with your right foot touching the end of a brick wall, waist high, with the understanding that you are going to coil the whole left side toward the wall during the backswing. If you tried to turn you would simply twist or spin (turning against the left hip joint) and the upper body would move away from the wall. You want to coil the upper body toward the wall, as deeply as you can, while maintaining the brace of the right leg.

If you went to the outside of the right foot in making this move, you would both lose the brace of the leg and send the upper body over the plane of the wall. Frankly, I wish I had students initially moving over the wall (I don't think I've seen six beginners move over the wall in 20 years) rather than turning *away* from it as is so common. If a student moves over the wall, he or she at least has a feeling for attempting to coil or move behind the ball, and we can realize immediate improvement by simply bracing up the right leg.

Those of you who follow the game closely may be aware of the fact that Ben Crenshaw's swing has been criticized in this respect. Crenshaw realizes that he moves through the brace of the right leg on occasion, and I know he is giving the problem attention. However, in Ben's defense, let me say this. If Crenshaw had spent his golfing life going *away* from the wall on his backswing he would be just another insurance agent in Austin—we wouldn't know his name!

The whole idea is to coil as deeply as you can, toward the wall, while making certain that your weight is on the inside of the right foot, leg and hip joint. Don't misunderstand this. I didn't say that the weight is on the right hip joint, or high on the right hip joint, but on the inside of the right hip joint. I stress this because of an unfortunate experience I had with J.C. Snead several years ago. J.C. has, in my estimation, one of the exceptional swings in golf. In talking with him about the move behind the ball, at some point we miscommunicated. Perhaps it was my fault, I really don't know. He interpreted my instruction in this area as suggesting a move back and up, high on the right hip, as opposed to coiling into the inside of the right hip joint. When players do this, they lose the flex in the right knee which must be preserved, and invariably move weight to the outside of the right foot, destroying the leg brace. From this position, as we shall see later, a golfer cannot recoil from the ground up and release properly.

The bracing of the legs creates an opposing feeling from the waist down. There is equal pressure on the inside of each leg. This feeling must never be destroyed. It would be like coiling a spring that was attached to the ground. You are taking your hand and coiling the upper part of the spring as tightly as you can against the fixed resistance of the lower part so that you create the strongest possible recoiling action when you release the spring. Because of the design of a spring, you could simply turn it to create the recoil. However, the human anatomy is infinitely more complicated than the spring, and if we are going to create a coiling and recoiling action, this action, as we have seen, involves more than we generally mean when we think of turning.

"But," you are saying, "if I coil toward the wall, won't I be moving off the ball? Won't I sway?" The answer is no. In fact, the biggest problem is that most golfers have such an ingrained fear of moving off the ball or swaying, that they actually sway forward. The word "sway" has been used improperly for years. Jimmy Demaret, in analyzing Ben Hogan's swing, once said, "Ben sways a

Right Side Power

If you were asked to budge a golf cart from its parked position using only the power you could generate with your right hand, as above, you would instinctively swing your hand into the cart seat with the same right-sided motion that is used in the golf swings of the great strikers of the ball. If you tried to "left-side" the cart into motion, nothing would happen.

little as he moves back, which I think most good golfers do—he moves back to right of center at the top of his swing." It's interesting that Demaret not only recognized the move to the right, he condoned it; but he still had to call it a sway. Hogan didn't sway. He coiled the entire left side into the brace or set of the right leg. He never moved away from the wall—that would be a sway forward. And he never moved through the brace of the right leg and over the ball—that would be a sway.

Your next question might be, "Well, if I'm not swaying, will my head be moving on the backswing?" The answer is that the head simply follows the spine as the player coils back to the top. The extent of head movement depends solely on where the player sets the head relative to the position of the ball at address.

Many teachers today recognize the necessity of moving behind the ball, and presumably to alleviate problems such as the ones we've just discussed (swaying and moving off the ball) they teach a set-up in which the head is positioned over the right knee and approximately 70 per cent of the weight is placed on the right foot. The idea is that now all the player has to do is move back to the head and then to the left.

This approach, although it sounds perfectly logical, is loaded with potential danger. Where an individual golfer places his head at address has a great deal to do with optics—that is, where he most naturally sees the ball.

Generally, although there are exceptions, if the right eye is the master eye, the player will be more comfortable with his head level and centered in the body, which will position it only slightly behind the ball.

If the left eye is the master, the player may cock or rotate the head to the right, and be quite comfortable with the head set considerably to the right at address. Hogan, for instance, wore a hole in the top of the left shoulder of his golf shirts while practicing because his shoulder rubbed against his chin as he coiled into the backswing. In watching Snead, the observer will definitely see that his head floats nicely with the spine, moving a little to the right as he coils. Nicklaus sets his head to the right and then rotates it a little farther to trigger his swing.

However, and this is the real point, all the great ball strikers coil back to the right. You must wind to unwind. A boxer couldn't set his weight on his right foot and then draw back his arm and throw a punch that would stagger his grandmother. And a baseball player can't just set his weight and the bat back to the right and move forward without hitting little popcorn jobs that could hardly back up an infielder. Natural rhythm and coordination, the obvious dynamics of hitting an object properly, dictate that the boxer, hitter or golfer coil and recoil in order to obtain leverage and power.

Where Hogan, Snead and Nicklaus set the head at address is predicated on personal comfort and where each man naturally sees the ball the best. If you convinced Hogan to move his head over his right knee or Nicklaus to stop rotating his head to the right, neither one would probably break 80! If you make a conscious effort to keep the head still, you are going to turn or twist, retard center and sway forward. On the other hand, if you make a conscious effort to move the head to the right, you are taking a chance of moving too far right, through the brace, and over the wall.

Setting up behind the ball is permissible if it does not violate an individual's optics and comfort. However, I have seen many players begin from this position and then sway forward away from the wall. The human body is always seeking equilibrium. Without our conscious intervention it wants to be balanced. Whether it's a child walking a fence rail or a world-class gymnast on a balance beam, if the equilibrium is temporarily threatened by too much body weight moving to one side there will be an unconscious natural thrust in the opposite direction in an attempt to retain the balanced centered feeling.

If a player sets up with 70 per cent of the weight on the right foot and starts the swing, at some point on the way back his balance and center will move to the left placing too much weight on the left foot, which would be a sway forward and the thing we have been trying to avoid above all—reverse pivoting. This may be simply defined as any kind of disconnection during the course of the backswing that caused center to stop or drop and leaves the player at the top, with his balance on his left foot or toe, that is, in front of the ball. The sway forward, away from the wall, not only destroys a player's potential power by preventing the correct coiling move behind the ball, but it also insures that the club cannot be returned square to the ball at impact on the intended line of flight.

There is one easy way of creating a big picture of this problem that has helped students avoid the various forms of disconnection discussed above. Suppose I asked you to take a braced connected address position without a club in your hand. Once you're set, I drive a golf cart up in front of you, and park it, so that the back cushion of the passenger seat is approximately opposite your left leg and close enough that you can easily hit it with either hand. I slip the gear shift into neutral, and ask you to hit the cart seat with your right hand . . . adding that if you can hit it hard enough to move the cart, I'll give you $20.

How would you do it? Or better yet, for the purposes of this discussion, how would you *not* do it? Well, if you like money, you wouldn't twist or turn the body under a stationary head moving to the left as you swung your arm back, and then lean to the right as you delivered the blow. If you did, you wouldn't even square up the palm of your hand against the back of the seat; you'd hardly depress the foam in the cushion, let alone move the cart.

Later, when we talk about the firing of the right side and the finish position, I'll show you how to hit the cart seat correctly, and why the great ball strikers never finish in a reverse "C" or bow position. One reason is that they never approximate a "C" position on the back-swing, instead they coil toward the wall with the upper body moving back and level. If there is even a hint of a "C" in the backswing, the player has reverse-pivoted, and left the upcoming shot in the lap of the gods.

When golfers reverse-pivot on the backswing, they automatically unload the gun. Since they arrive at the top with the weight predominantly on the left foot or toe, it must move to the right foot during the down-swing. In other words, the reverse-pivoter changes directions in the backswing. It is impossible to shift weight to the left, when it is already there! With the disconnection and the tilt forward, the opportunity to coil behind the ball has been destroyed, all leverage and resistance leaves the legs, and all of the large muscles of the legs and body are immobilized.

The failure to coil into the inside of the right leg and hip joint prevents the proper, sequential recoiling from the ground up, and the player has no option but to begin the swing from the top—that is, with the smaller muscles of the hands and arms. As the hips are simply spinning and, in fact, the weight is transferring to the right foot, the player throws or casts the club from the top—an out and over feeling—which forces the path of the swing to be across the intended line of flight. Generally, the player drags the club across the ball with the face open and hits a weak slice. When this is done to any degree, the player can sense the absence of solid, square contact, he feels he has hit the ball a sort of glancing blow. We call it a "wipe." However, from exactly the same beginnings, the player might occasionally flip the hands over and hit a dead pull. We can illustrate this simply in photographs looking down the intended line with the "Look Mom . . . no hands" shot (see illustration, page 130). When the golfer throws, drops or drags from the top of the swing across the intended line, the hands will disappear in the impact area. They have been pulled out of the center of the chest.

The same disconnection that produced the slice, pull and top in most high handicappers' games will not be so pronounced in the ailing swing of a better player. If he reverses going back, it won't be as drastic. Some weight may get to the right side and be transferred. It's all a matter of degree. The better player may experience pushed shots and a loss of distance, interspersed with a few quick hooks. The path of the club is not quite so bad, but disconnection at some point is preventing the player from squaring the face of the club to the ball at impact. Generally, the shot will feel weak, and the player will complain of an inability to release through the ball. This is described as a block. We saw in the exercise in which we placed the club in the center of the chest that, at waist-high through the ball, the left arm begins to fold on the body and the right arm almost immediately covers the left, obscuring it from view as seen from the straight-on camera angle. We also see the identical position in the swings of the great ball strikers at this point.

However, on a blocked shot, we will see disconnection (unplugging) at the left shoulder; the right side has not been released from the ground up; and you can see daylight between the arms. This is the same picture as the "disappearing hands," but taken from the front. Visually, you get the feeling that center has been restricted, or momentarily stopped, which has caused the arms to run wide on the through swing, making it impossible to square the club to the ball. This is in fact what happened. The player's feelings are not sabotaging him. He feels no release because none is there. Shortly, we will put the reasons for this in total perspective. But for the moment, we must realize that blocking is an effect, not a cause.

The Band-aid remedy for blocking would be the suggestion that you "get the hands in faster." Here's an error to offset an error. If you don't do anything about the blocking action itself, and only flip the hands, you're going to lose a lot of balls in the left woods. In golf, two wrongs inevitably make a wrong. Somewhere, perhaps as far back as the address position, disconnection has taken place, and then been multiplied into a block. Instead of grasping for straws like hand manipulation, a golfer must check his address position, triangle and center, and move behind the ball and his connections. Only then will he be able to isolate the real cause of the problem.

Reverse-pivoting, wiping and blocking are not faults restricted to the average player. They creep into the games of touring pros, and bring prolonged periods of frustration. A pro who's blocking the ball might look pretty good to the untrained eye of the weekender, but at his competitive level it doesn't take many blocks to wipe out a payday.

One of the most interesting cases of reverse-pivoting and blocking I've ever witnessed involved the man recognized as one of the tour's longest hitters. In 1978, Jim Dent was playing poorly. He told me his problems had started with some wildness, and that other pros had suggested that he hold back on the power and work on control. In attempting to do this, he had ultimately lost both power and accuracy. We went out, and I took some pictures of his swing. In trying to control the ball, Dent had become hand- and arm-conscious and developed a reverse pivot. Now he couldn't hit it long at all by tour standards.

I remember saying to Jim, before we discussed his problem and looked at the pictures, that I didn't buy the power-versus-accuracy premise. When a golfer, at any ability level, is playing his best, he is striking a high percentage of all shots squarely, and is therefore on the average both his longest and straightest.

I showed Jim his reverse pivot and the subsequent block on the video. We discussed the solution—making sure he coiled deeply behind the ball into the brace of the right leg. I remember his reaction: "What you're saying is, when I swing the club back the ammunition falls out of my gun." I agreed with that, and we left for the driving range. He hit some irons and improved immediately. That afternoon, he hauled out the driver to put the coil to the acid test. My driving range is about 270 yards long with teeing area on both ends. We were on the lower end and Jim was hitting uphill. Behind the tee on the upper end is a stand of trees. Beyond the trees is a cart path, practice putting green, and the 18th green. Then there's another cart path, and the 10th fairway, and then another cart path and my house. After he hit the third tee shot, I checked the practice putting green. Mac McLendon said later, "I was chipping onto the 18th when the shelling started!" After he'd hit ten balls I wondered if my wife and our dog were locked in the house shaking. Homero Blancas, Bill Kratzert, Gary Groh, Bobby Walzel, and Bunky Henry stopped hitting balls and filtered over to observe. After Jim hit the tenth ball, I saw McLendon making his way back toward us in a cart. After the 15th, Dent paused, turned slowly toward me with a wide smile on his face and said, "Well, Captain ...now I got me some bullets!" While everybody was nodding agreement, Mac drove up with a sheepish grin on his face. "Jim...could you aim just a little more left...I'm trying to practice my chipping...about 340 yards from here!"

Before we move on to the change of direction and the downswing, I want to stress some further aspects of positioning and center as they relate to the coiling move behind the ball.

Once a player has assumed the braced connected address position, he has in essence created his backswing plane. The knees and hips should always be level and the backswing plane is dictated by the vertical tilt forward of the spine, and the plane of the shoulders thus created. The old arguments about upright and flat backswing planes are meaningless. Neither is fundamentally correct or incorrect. Once the plane of the shoulders and arms is set at address and the club is coiled back with connection, the golfer can't help but be on the proper plane regardless of what we call it.

Hogan and Nicklaus represent the practical limits between the so-called flat and upright backswing planes. But both men do exactly the same thing. Once the plane of the shoulders is established at address neither man varies that plane during the backswing. Once the shoulder plane is established, they maintain that level to the top of the backswing.

Earlier, I said that during the backswing, center coils back and slightly up. As you're sitting in the chair, you can move center up, marginally, by taking a deep breath, or raising this book up above your head. What we are really trying to do is make the knees, hips, center and shoulders coil back level, or on their respective planes, just as Hogan and Nicklaus do.

I would never stress center going up unless a player were dropping it as he swung back. In this case, suggesting that he move center up would be an attempt to get such a player to move it *level*. Actually if a player makes a fetish of trying to get center up, he'll pull his right shoulder through the top of the shoulder plane, straighten the right leg, destroy his brace, and create unwanted wideness of the arms. The key is to coil the triangle with center into the brace of the right leg while maintaining the respective levels of the knees, hips, center and shoulders established in the braced connected address position.

At the top of the backswing, the weight should be on the inside of the right foot, and right hip and the balance point should be six to eight inches behind the ball. Try to exaggerate the coiling motion—to go as deep as you possibly can with connection, and without the weight going to the outside of the right foot or hip. I suggest this because I know from experience that unless you make a definite point of it, you will cut the coiling short, and come up with some degree of twist and a reverse. In Demaret's words, I want you to "sway" like Hogan.

If you're still a little hesitant to coil to the right,

consider this. Imagine we drive center all the way through the body to the base of the spine, and swing with our attention focused on the spine as the axis. Looking at it this way, the upper body coil that may have appeared excessive when viewed from center as the middle of the chest, is reduced to a lateral movement so small as to be inconsequential.

COMMON DENOMINATOR 3 The golfer must coil the triangle and center behind the ball into the brace of the right leg.

CHAPTER SEVEN

THE CHANGE OF DIRECTION

T he sole purpose of coiling the triangle into the brace of the right leg with connection is to create the strongest possible position from which to reverse the direction of the club and make it recoil squarely into the back of the ball.

Most teachers agree that the downswing must be initiated with the feet and legs, but from this point on, students encounter contradiction rather than clarity. So let's look closely at what actually happens during the transition period between the backswing and the downswing.

Here's an analogy that should provide a feeling for the whole sensation. Visualize a fisherman casting with a fly rod. While the rod and line are behind him, something has to change the direction and move them forward. To a casual observer, that something might appear to be the arm. But could a fisherman produce a long accurate cast if he were standing on a slippery mud bank, using just his arm? Absolutely not. A strong reversal would have to begin from the ground and proceed up through the body. That's the reason the great golfer braces his legs and literally grips the ground with his feet. With the golf club, as with the fly rod, reversal must be an immediate, natural, and coordinated response to the coiling action, and it must start from ground level.

On any practice tee, golfers can be seen trying to set the club at the top of the swing. Some even stop and look—presumably checking the plane of the swing, the relationship to parallel, and the position of the clubface relative to open, closed or square. From our discussion thus far, it should be obvious that a player can't possibly do this without disconnecting entirely. (In this regard, I've had the thought that it's unfortunate that club shafts are stiffer than fishing line, because if the club fell on the ground behind golfers as a result of this activity, they'd quit trying it.)

Part of the confusion also may stem from the old instructional saw, "swing the club up and down in the same path." Never has a decent golfer done this. It can be seen in the swings of any of the great ball strikers that there is an upswing plane and a downswing plane and the upswing plane is always more vertical than the downswing plane.

So: the correct position at the top is achieved with the reverse of the legs. The transition from the completion of the backswing to the start of the downswing is created by a kick of the right foot and right knee toward the ball. It is this move that allows the club to "fall in" on its correct downswing plane. There is no conscious attempt to do anything with the hands and arms.

While many golfers hurt their swings by fiddling with the positions at the top, others have done damage consciously trying to pause at the completion of the backswing. The appearance of a pause in many of the swings of the great ball strikers is simply that fraction of a second when the right foot and right knee kick toward the ball precipitating the plane change and the fall-in. In reality, all of the great strikers begin the kick of the right foot while the upper body is still coiling back. For this reason, it is extremely difficult to delineate exactly where the backswing stops, and the downswing starts.

But as a practical matter, the question is not only moot, but dangerous. Avoid any notion that you complete the backswing as a separate entity, and then start the downswing as something else. It doesn't work this way. In the good golf swing, there is a connected and simultaneous aspect to what is happening.

COMMON DENOMINATOR #4 The golfer must reverse the club with the right foot and right knee to create the proper position at the top.

Reversing the direction of the club in order to make it recoil squarely into the back of the ball is an action that must be initiated with the lower body—specifically with a kick of the right foot and knee toward the ball— and not with the hands and arms. Notice how in the Hogan sequence the clubhead has continued dropping after the right knee kicks to start the backswing. Hands and arms remain controlled by the large muscles of the legs and torso as the downswing begins.

Imagine casting a fly rod from a slippery mud bank— if you threw with just your hands you would fall off balance. But if you remained braced and connected to the ground, and initiated the cast from the legs, as shown, the "line" on your fly rod would fall in, then move out toward your target with momentum and accuracy.

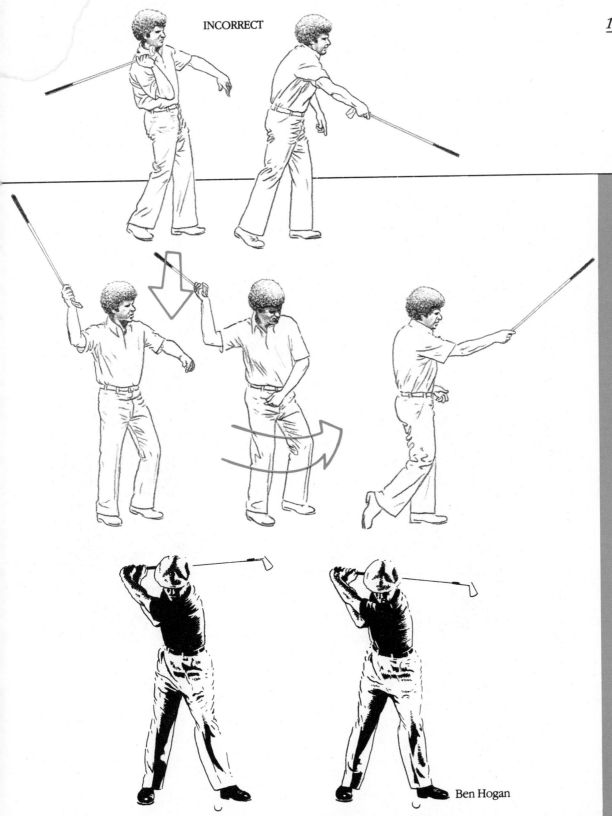

INCORRECT

Ben Hogan

Proof Of Connection Power

"Springing" or bending the shaft at the onset of the downswing is visible proof of the kind of force created by a swing that emanates from the ground up. Notice how Tom Watson's right foot, right knee, right side and center itself have changed in the two frames. The bow in the shaft is the result of a connected process involving the entire body.

All we have been discussing thus far has been a coiled connected position on the inside of the right foot, so that at the top of the swing the right foot, right knee and right side want to recoil naturally and strongly through the ball. Our task, providing the backswing is correct, is really no task at all. But if we've gone away from the wall, we've already changed directions. If we went through the brace and over the wall our weight is now on the outside of the right foot and we can't initiate action with the right foot and right knee. And if we try to make a conscious pause, we'll kill the accumulated energy which is built up during the connected coiling of the backswing.

It boils down to two choices. Doing it correctly with a connected swing produces the casual build-up that will all but make it happen. Disconnection in the form of an arm swing from the shoulder joints, a reverse pivot or a contrived pause will force you to cast the club from the top.

Generally, when I ask a student on the lesson tee to show me what is meant by releasing in the golf swing, he will stand flat-footed and flip his hands through the hitting area. Most golfers perceive the release as purely the function of the wrists and hands. They understand it as a somewhat disconnected activity of the smaller muscles of the body. Instead, release is a process involving primarily the large muscles of the body, starting with the connected change of direction.

Photos of the great ball strikers show that they create enough centrifugal force to bow or spring the shaft immediately as the club assumes the downswing plane, and maintain this pressure on the shaft through the impact area. In the swings of poorer players this phenomenon is drastically reduced or totally absent. Why? Because it is impossible to create centrifugal force if you simply pull or drag the club toward the ball with a disconnected move of the arms and hands.

The law of centrifugal force dictates a stable center or midpoint from which the energy can be built up and then passed and multiplied to the perimeter. If you swing a rock on a tether about your head, you can increase the speed of the rock as long as you maintain a reasonably steady hand position. But if you interrupt the sequence by jerking your hand to one side, you lose the stored energy and the centrifugal relationship. If in the Bible story David had been interrupted or distracted in the middle of his assault on Goliath he would have been turned into ground-under-repair by the big guy.

In the golf swing, when you achieve a coiled position behind the ball at the top of the backswing, the kick of the right foot and right knee begins a connected chain reaction which is transmitted from the ground up, through your body center and on out through arms, hands and club. If you recoil from the feet upward, preserving every element of connection in the process, you will have achieved maximum efficiency of movement, and prevented any part of the anatomy from operating independently of any other.

We cannot bend or "spring" the shaft of our club by consciously directing arms and hands to do it, any more than we can create power by consciously pulling down with the butt of the club. That is a case of trying to make our small muscles do the impossible. But if the club has been coiled properly and with connection, reversal becomes an immediate, natural and coordinated response to the coiling action. Then arms and hands will automatically release through impact, allowing the golfer to literally explode through the hitting area in a strong, controlled, but free-wheeling fashion.

Another way of understanding the true source of shaft-springing power is to assume your braced connected address position at home or office so you can place the head of the club squarely against a door jamb. Now, using hands, wrists and arms only, see how much pressure you can put on the shaft by pushing forward. A little but not much. But try it by driving your right foot and knee—incorporating all of the large muscles of the body—as you would in the proper position of the golfer at impact. From here you should feel that you could almost snap the shaft.

Every golfer talks about the occasional near-perfect shot in which the swing felt unhurried, there was a definite sensation of accumulated clubhead speed, the ball jumped off the clubface, and the stroke finished fully and effortlessly. In a connected swing, when the player learns to move behind the ball, changes the direction of the club with a kick of the right foot and right knee followed immediately by the continued releasing of the whole right side and center, the feelings set out above become the norm rather than accidental exceptions.

COMMON DENOMINATOR 4 The golfer must reverse the club with the right foot and right knee to create the proper position at the top of the swing.

CHAPTER EIGHT

FIRING THE RIGHT SIDE

F or the past two decades, I've had some idea of how Galileo felt in the 1500's when he suggested the world was round—only to have the religious establishment introduce him to the thumbscrew.

Teaching the firing of the right side has proven to be the most controversial area of my instructional approach. On virtually every lesson tee in America, the right side is considered the golfer's arch enemy. For as long as anyone can remember, it has been incorrectly accused of overpowering the left side. The product of this long-standing fallacy has been strict emphasis on the left-side control doctrine, and the insistence that the right side play a totally submissive role. Let's take a moment to investigate the myth of the right side overpowering the left.

There are basically three ways that a player can experience feelings, during the swing, that might lead him to conclude that either the right side was taking over or, as some say, the left side was breaking down. The three are: (1) reverse pivoting, (2) failure to initiate the downswing with the legs, or from the ground up, and (3) "hit anxiety."

When we discussed reverse pivoting earlier, we saw that if a player sways away from the wall, he changes directions immediately, destroying the opportunity to coil behind the ball into the strongest hitting position. Without coiling into the brace of the right leg, he has disconnected the interrelationship of the large muscles and therefore must initiate the downswing with the hands and arms. This creates the out- and over-the-top feeling, and the player incorrectly rationalizes this as the right hand, arm and side overpowering the left. Here again we run into confusion as to cause and effect. The cause of the improper chain reaction was the reverse pivot which placed the weight on the left foot in the beginning of the swing. The player unloaded the gun at the outset, and this disconnection forced the arms and hands to initiate the downswing from the top. The feeling that the right hand and side attempted to take over was an effect. The reverse pivot underpowered the swing immediately, and forced the right side to attempt to salvage the shot.

Presuming that the player has coiled properly behind the ball, he must then reverse the club with the legs—from the ground up. As we shall see, if he fails to initiate the swing with the right foot and right knee, but goes top side, and starts the swing by pulling the arms down, he will never move his balance to the left, and may well conclude from the feelings experienced that his hands and arms have taken command. They have! And since his right arm is the strongest it will inevitably be blamed for the takeover. Cause and effect problems again. In this instance, the failure to initiate with the legs caused the player to hang back on the right side. He didn't drive with the feet and legs; therefore the proper chain reaction prevented the upper body from releasing center. The effect has the arms and hands racing by center as the body lays back on the lazy right side.

Hit anxiety requires little explanation. It is trying to drive the ball 290 yards when your average tee shot goes 215. Here, your ego overpowers your common sense and reduces any semblance of rhythm, coordination, and connection to an absolute shambles. In this case, temporary stupidity overpowered rationality, and blaming the right side is no more than reflexive ignorance. In all three instances we have classic examples of the tail trying to wag the dog.

Teaching right-handed golfers to attempt to control

the club exclusively with the left side reminds me of the outdated practice of forcing left-handed schoolchildren to learn to write right-handed—and in its own way, it may have caused some significant long-term learning disabilities among the golfing public. Of two things I am absolutely certain: (1) There has never been a great striker of the ball who didn't tear at it with the right side, and (2) the right side is the most valuable untapped resource that the average golfer possesses. Therefore, unless it is absolutely necessary—and it definitely isn't—why should a golfer relegate the control of the swing to the weaker side?

When John McKay coached O.J. Simpson in football at the University of Southern California, he was asked, "Why, when you have several premier running backs, do you run O.J. as many as 45 times a game?" Coach McKay's answer: "When I was a boy, my father told me, 'Son, if you have a big gun, shoot it!' " I'll buy that, and add, as a golfer you have a potentially powerful ally in the right side. I suggest that you learn to fire it!

Using the right side to initiate the downswing may awaken some comfortable and natural feelings that have been dormant since the days of physical education classes and the playground. Golf has the reputation of "making Christians out of more ex-jocks than any other game in the western world." If this is true, I believe the answer lies in the fact that some of the most logical and natural elements of rhythm and coordination failed to leave school when the players did.

Along these lines, one of the most interesting teaching experiences I've had involved a modern-day distaff equivalent of my original teacher, Sam Byrd. Joan Joyce is recognized as the finest female softball pitcher in the world. She can throw a softball 118 mph at 44 feet and

Lee Trevino

COMMON DENOMINATOR #5

The golfer *must*, after initiating the change of direction with the right foot and right knee, immediately release the entire right side and center, insuring that the triangle returns to the original position squaring the club to the ball at impact.

The triangle of the arms and shoulders is intact at the moment of impact for Trevino, Knudson, Snead and all great strikers of the ball, showing that a total release of power from body center has occurred. The down-the-line view of Trevino demonstrates particularly well how much "right side" gets into a truly effective downswing. The release of stored-up energy is achieved from the ground up.

The sequence shows a drill to train arms and hands in the passive role they must play. Grip the club with your hands about 4″ apart and slowly swing back and through a number of times being sure to maintain the arms-shoulders triangle. You should become aware of how the hands complement each other in their roles throughout—while one pulls, the other pushes with an equal force, and vice versa. Also you should notice that the clubface squares up through the impact area without your manipulating the hands in any way.

George Knudson

Sam Snead

when her schedule permits, she competes on the LPGA tour. When Joan first came to me, she had already worked with a teacher who stressed left side control. Initially we discussed what actually happens in the golf swing and compared the moves we could see in the swings of the great ball strikers to the moves we could see in the swings of exceptional baseball hitters. Fine hitters dig a hole with the right foot, and create what is tantamount to a miniature starting block in track. They then coil center far behind the intended point of contact—deep into the brace of the right leg. As the pitcher nears delivery, they coil a little deeper and literally explode off of the right side. The hitter is also a study in connection. Viewed from above we could see the operation of the triangle. The left arm is against the chest, and the right arm assumes the natural strong position away from the body. When the ball is struck the end of the bat is pointing at the center of the chest. If the hitter reaches for a bad pitch, we have run-off. The arms disconnect, grow longer, and work independently of the torso. When this happens, the hitter experiences a loss of balance, and the ball may go out of the park, but not far, and not between the foul lines.

We also discussed the balance points in the golf swing and likened those to baseball. Hitters coil the center of the chest to a position directly above the right knee and their balance point is approximately eight inches be hind the intended point of contact. Instantly, when they commit and take their stride, the balance point moves to the left foot eight to ten inches in front of the intended point of contact.

The golfer does essentially the same thing. At the top of the backswing, center has been coiled to a place directly over the knee of the braced right leg, and the

Right Is Might
Sometimes when Gary Player is playing well, he actually steps through his shots with his right leg, as shown. If you want to experience right-side performance, try doing the same while hitting balls on the practice range.

player's balance point is six to eight inches behind the ball. But as soon as the right foot and right knee kick, the player moves immediately to the left foot and the balance point is six to eight inches past the ball. Accomplished golfers take what might be called a stride, or step, in place. Gary Player bothers the traditional purists who insist he loses his balance when he steps totally through shots after impact. In 1977, he stepped through shots for three weeks, and won three tournaments, including the Masters. He was losing his balance the same way Hogan swayed! Player was simply firing his right side so hard that he was forced to step through his shots. For years, I've had players who want to hang back on the right side, step through their shots on the lesson tee, as a feel drill to activate the sense of firing the right side.

Back to Joan. As soon as she focused her attention on the right side and compared the recognizable and natural similarities in pitching and batting to the observable realities in the golf swing she realized immediate and significant improvement. A month or so later, I heard from her: "Golf is so much better—wish I had more time to work on it. My batting average has gone up 20 points—unheard of for a pitcher!" Without belaboring the issue, I hope I'm making the point: most golfers have followed advice which has effectively "benched" their most active and naturally stronger side.

If you are still wary of changing your perspective from left to right in initiating the downswing, I want to emphasize the following:

> If a golfer has coiled 70 to 80 percent of the weight into the inside of the right foot, right leg and right hip joint at the top of the backswing...
> how can he or she possibly initiate the downswing with the left side?

Right Side Firepower
Aerial view shows how golfer (figure above) loses power and ends up dragging club across the ball by sliding hips through the impact area. In the correct firing of the right side, the right knee drives toward and through ball, placing club on target line. Insets show knee action of Byron Nelson in his prime. Note how the all-time great drove his right knee in direction of ball, not down "inner rail" which would have produced a slice or push.

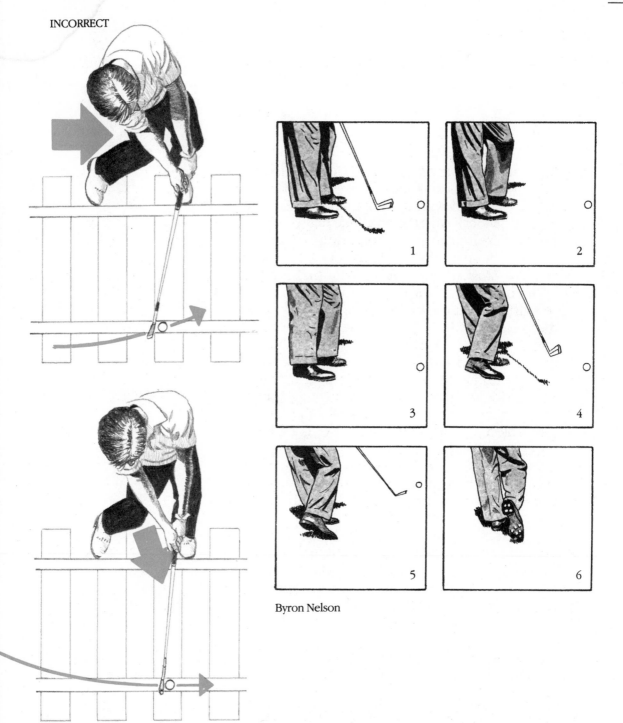

INCORRECT

1

2

3

4

5

6

Byron Nelson

I'll answer my own question: he can't! However, explanations of how this phase of the swing feels to particular individuals, coupled with the popular misconception, discussed previously, that the right side may overpower the left, have created no end of confusion.

Let's look at an example. Hogan, in his book *Five Lessons: The Modern Fundamentals of Golf,* said, "To begin the downswing, turn your hips back to the left. There must be enough lateral motion forward to transfer the weight to the left foot." He continued, "The contracted muscles along the inside of the left thigh start to spin the left hip around to the left. At one and the same time, the muscles of the right hip and right thigh— both the inside and the powerful outside thigh muscles —start to move the right hip forward." Eleven pages later, he stated, "As far as applying power goes, I wish I had three right hands!"

Let me digress a moment. Hogan obviously felt the initiating of the swing in the mid-body area rather than in the feet. This is why I may have to try 10 to 15 different ways to get a player to feel a particular move. I've got to find that player's particular area of what we might call anatomical response. Teaching of such feel is and will remain the most challenging area of golf instruction.

Over the years, I've become firmly convinced that language suggesting that a player either spin or turn the hips carries with it grave potential danger. This was Hogan's assessment of how he both conceived and felt the sensations as his downswing began. Several other great players have felt and expressed this aspect of the swing in much the same manner. When I read this, however, I am reading connection. When golfers talk about initiating the swing with, or hitting against a strong left side, they are experiencing a connected left side—

that's why it feels strong. If the right side fires, the left hip has to unwind and get out of the way. But if players attempt to consciously initiate the downswing by either turning the left hip out of the way or moving the knees laterally to the left, they inevitably spin or slide. If I've seen it once, I've seen it a thousand times. By concentrating on turning the left hip, or sliding the knees laterally, a player will pull the club across the intended line on every shot.

Suppose we set ourselves up, on a railroad track as shown in the illustration on page 127. We assume the braced connected address position with the feet on the inner rail and the ball on the outer rail which represents the intended line of flight toward the target. Presuming a standard full shot with the ball placed opposite the left heel, our intention is to return the club from the inside down the intended line, squaring the face to the back of the ball with maximum velocity at impact. This can only happen if the initial direction of movement is toward and through the ball, and not lateral or around. When the right foot and right knee kick, followed immediately by the whole right side releasing toward the ball and to a point past it, the hands respond by falling into the proper set position behind us, and they will then be released on the correct plane, from the inside down the line. In essence, the firing of the right side extends the club down the line of flight. The right shoulder, center and arm release as the natural sequential response to the lower body activity, just as they would if we were pitching a ball strongly from the address position. As the right arm extends down the outer rail, the left arm must begin to fold up on the body. If we make an effort to extend both arms, we will unplug at the left shoulder, force the right arm under the left and create a block.

Tom Weiskopf

INCORRECT

Releasing

Tom Weiskopf (left) has fired the entire right side and center which in turn releases the arms and hands squarely through the impact area and down the target line. As the club approaches waist high on the follow-through the 'toe is in the air' and the butt of the club in body center.

The golfer at right has not fired the entire right side and center. Center has 'dropped' and the arms have been 'pulled' across the intended target line and out of sight from this camera angle. The upper body (center) was not fully released and consequently neither were the arms and hands. The clubface is open, and the shot is 'blocked' or 'wiped'. As opposed to squaring the blade at impact on the intended line, this golfer has struck it a glancing blow.

Suppose a player slides both knees laterally down the rail he's standing on? By doing this, he is "softening" the right side rather than driving with it. The slide creates a drop of center and puts the club into the improper position, and since the initial direction of movement is down the same rail the feet are on, the club will be dragged across the line of flight. This is no more than lateral movement without the requisite uncoiling on the downswing.

On the other hand, if the player simply turns the hips, we reverse the process, but arrive at the same practical results. Turning only, or spinning the hips as it's commonly called, is a weakened attempt to uncoil, with a total absence of lateral movement. Again, as with sliding, when players simply turn the hips it is impossible for the club to fall into the proper set position behind them and thus be released inside and down the intended line. A spinning body results in the club being thrown out and over so that the swing path is also across the line of flight. Understanding and learning to fire the right side fuses together automatically the correct degree of lateral movement and unwinding, the proper mix of actions that appears in the downswings of the great ball strikers.

Although I discussed the change of direction separately in the earlier section, I did so because I wanted to definitely steer the reader away from two disastrous thoughts: (1) that the backswing and downswing can be treated separately, and (2) that the golfer can make anything beneficial happen by stopping or manipulating the club in any way at the top of the swing. However, we could really say that the firing of the right side begins with the right foot and right knee.

Let me make two distinctions in this area. I always

refer to the initial move of the right foot as a "kick." The concept of "pushing" suggests a slower transfer than we're attempting to create. In a connected sequence, we want to shoot our balance from the inside of the braced right leg, to and past the ball as quickly as possible. A golfer can't leisurely recoil, or he'll invariably leave too much weight on the right foot, retard center and hang back. Also, be absolutely sure that you do not kick the knee *behind* the ball. Remember, the right knee should feel as if you are kicking it *toward* the ball and *past it* down the outside rail toward the target.

To create a feel sense for the kick of the right foot and knee, followed by the immediate sequential releasing of the whole right side and center, let us return to our example of striking a cart seat. Remember that I offered $20 to a reverse-pivoter if he could hit the seat hard enough to move the cart? Now, how would you actually do it if you wanted my money?

In the first place, you would not twist or turn as you drew your right arm back. You would coil your upper body, from the lat muscles, as deeply as you could while maintaining the brace of the legs. You would then fire your right side, from the ground up, literally tearing at it with a connected right side, so that you contacted the cart seat flush with the palm of the hand and maximum power. You would have the definite sensation of firing up and leveling, because if you allowed the upper body and center to hang back you would obviously rob yourself of potential power. You should feel your leg muscles, the insides of the calves and the thigh muscles all the way into the muscles of the posterior tighten and drive up. The right arm would maintain the connected position from which it started. If it disconnected, and moved independently, you would instantly negate all of

---

Releasing

Many players feel that the right forearm crosses *over* the left following impact, but as this Jack Nicklaus sequence reveals, the right hand and arm stay on the outside of the track of the ball throughout. The right forearm must never move under the left (see figure below at left), or you will produce a block slice or push. So also, if the right forearm crosses over the left (below at right), you will create a duck hook.

Jack Nicklaus

INCORRECT

INCORRECT

the good work of the larger muscles of the body and turn the entire process into an ineffectual arm-slapping of the cart seat. Also notice that as you strike the seat the right hand is in line with the center of the chest. If you can both feel and fully appreciate what's being done in this example, my money is in jeopardy. If you can transfer these ideas to your golf swing, the money of your future opponents is in jeopardy!

Let's now repeat the exercise but change hands. We do this because some individuals more easily relate to feel sensations in the left side. From the same braced connected address, try and backhand the cart into motion. In this instance, you would immediately feel the connected left shoulder, both the pec and lat. You would then coil the left lat as deeply as you possibly could to the right, while preserving the brace of the right leg. And, although the individual who is more oriented to the left side would initiate with the right foot, the predominant feel might be one of the left hip and side driving level while at the same time unwinding on the inner rail as rapidly as is physically possible. Again, the backhander would not lay back with the upper body. If that happened, the left arm would disconnect (begin to unplug), because the upper body has not been released along with the legs, and as a result the butt or heel of the left hand as opposed to the back of the left would contact the cushion with diminishing force. But if the player squared up to the seat the left hand would be directly opposite the center of the chest and the weight would be completely transferred to the left foot.

The cart seat analogies not only serve as excellent feel sense drills to create the correct downswing sensations, they are also a near-perfect primer that should prepare golfers to understand both the true source of power in

COMMON DENOMINATOR #6 The golfer must, at waist high past the ball, have maintained the triangle with the belt buckle and center facing target.

Every great golfer maintains the arms-shoulders triangle at least until the club reaches waist level on the follow-through, long after the ball has shot off the face of the club. The butt of the club points at body center, which has uncoiled in the direction of the target.

Rehearse the correct feeling of the connected follow-through extending the forefinger of your right hand down the shaft and swinging back and through a few times. Done correctly (bottom figure), finger and club will point on target when you reach waist level. The triangle is lost when you "flip" or rotate your hands over through impact so that the finger points to the left of target (top view), or when you slice or block the shot so that the finger points to the right.

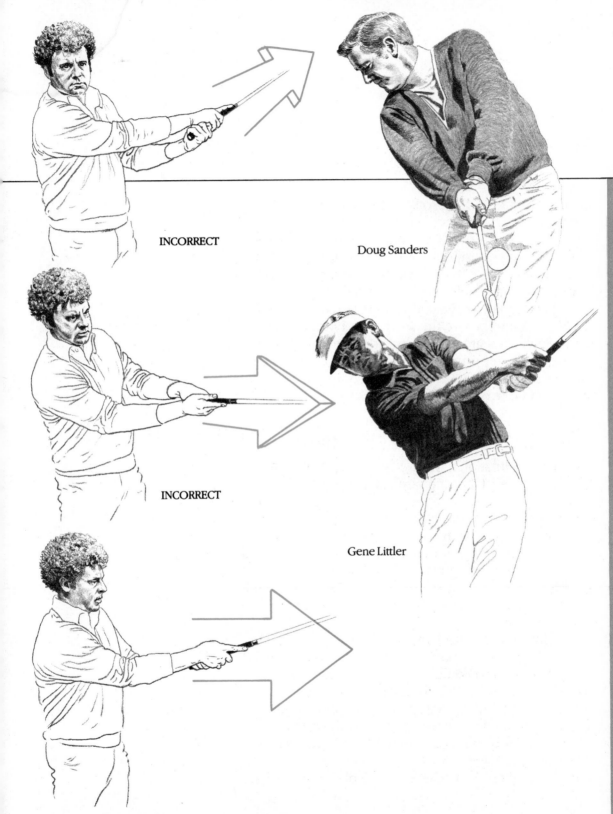

INCORRECT

Doug Sanders

INCORRECT

Gene Littler

the golf swing and the often-misunderstood area of releasing.

We can dispense with the source-of-power problem quickly. In my business I constantly hear stories about some guy who hit it from the fifth tee at such and such a course, over the clubhouse and down the road to a 7-11 store just this side of the county line. Usually, I've never heard his name before the story, and I'll never hear it again. Power is a great asset, but as someone once said, "It doesn't do any good to air-mail it if it doesn't have an address and zip code!" I'm interested only in accurate power, and that comes from the creation and maintaining of a connected golf swing.

UNDERSTANDING RELEASING

In lesson situations, when I deal with the subject of releasing, I encounter the same kinds of problems that we discussed earlier in the section on the triangle and center. We found there that players had difficulty with the one-piece takeaway because most instructors had limited the teaching of the move to hands, arms and shoulders. They had not taken it far enough, that is, into the body. The upshot of this was a hands-arms-and-shoulder-joints-takeaway that prompted an immediate disconnection.

Usually, asking a student to demonstrate his or her conception of the release in the golf swing is like asking, "Where is your shoulder?" The generally accepted notion of the release has the golfer's focus on the arms and hands. When I ask for an example of releasing, the student will stand flat-footed and swing the club open to closed, accentuating the move so that the right forearm crosses over the left.

It seems that most teachers and players who have

written about the game isolate how the arms and hands travel in the course of the swing in trying to explain the releasing action. What they show is not wrong, but in my opinion it leaves out the essential element. It invites the student to consider the arms and hands independently and in so doing violates the cardinal rule of connection.

In the golf swing, the hands and arms do release, but the body releases with them. This is the whole point of establishing and maintaining connection. When you tried to move the cart by striking the seat with either hand, what released the arm and hand? And when you struck the seat, where was the hand in relation to center? Why is the butt of the club pointing to center, with the triangle intact, at the moment of impact in the swings of all the great ball strikers?

The difference between the proper release and the improper release is the difference between connection and disconnection. When you fire the right side, and the connected left side unwinds out of the way, it permits center to release, and the continuance of connection insures that the club stays in the center of the chest and squares up to the ball at impact. There is the appearance in the immediate follow-through of the right arm crossing the left, and the right forearm in a feel sense does cross over. However, as we discussed in the areas on the triangle and blocking, the right forearm covers the left from the front view. Go back to our original exercise with the butt of the club in the center of the chest and experience the through swing again, paying particular attention to natural and proper arm rotation. Where are your arms? If you tried to cross over violently, you wouldn't be able to finish the swing above your shoulders. So, the right forearm must never move under the left—that creates a block. And the right forearm crossing over with the body staying back is simply a release of the hands and arms only, which results in ugly duck hooks.

When the higher handicapper tries consciously to release with the hands and arms, the practical results are usually a block slice or a severe pull. And the better player who restricts his view of releasing to the hands and arms will most certainly supinate himself into a siege of snap hooking. Releasing must be understood and applied in its direct relationship to the correct connected activity of the entire body. If it isn't, the golfer will turn a great game into a continual Easter Egg Hunt.

I am convinced that many of the great golfers have had an appreciation for both the efficiency of motion in the swing that I call connection and the proper conception of releasing. Hogan said, "The action of the arms is motivated by the movements of the body, and the hands consciously do nothing but maintain a firm grip on the club." Trevino dedicated his own book to Hogan, and has been quoted as saying that early in his career he watched Ben practice one afternoon and became convinced that "Hogan controlled his shots with his body." On a number of occasions, Nicklaus has alluded to Trevino's "syrupy smooth body action," as being perhaps the best on the tour, and so it goes.

The point I would like the reader to remember is this: Don't consider any movements of the hands and arms without keeping in mind the absolutely essential connecting elements of the body. If you do, you break the cardinal rule of connection by focusing attention on the independent activity of the smaller muscles. By doing this, you will almost certainly revert to a swinging action that makes you the hopeless prisoner of hand-arm dominance.

There are two more feel senses I would like you to consider in regard to the firing of the right side. For reasons that will become apparent, I am going to ask you to physically experience one, and use your imagination a little on the other. Several times I have mentioned the term "toe in the air is square." We have seen both in exercises and in the swings of the great ball strikers that when a player coils behind the ball the toe of his club is in the air at approximately waist-high on the backswing, square at impact, and that the toe is again in the air at approximately waist-high on the follow-through. In essence, the toe of the club can be visualized as "wrapping around" the ball in the process of traveling back and through. But it is wrapping around the ball as the result of a connected backswing and a totally connected release of the body which, in turn, releases the arms and hands. I call this process "covering the ball with the toe of the club." If a player coils behind the ball and fires the right side recoiling with connection, he or she will automatically square up to the ball and cover the shot. I have found it beneficial to suggest that players consciously try to produce the feeling that they are "covering" the shots they hit with connection.

I don't mean to imply that a player would flip the toe of the club over with the hands. I am saying that when you coil into the right side and fire it, it's the feeling that the toe of the club is wrapping around or covering the ball, and never the feeling of pulling the heel of the club at the ball. Also, consider this. Presuming the player has coiled behind the ball properly, he can fire as hard as he wants to, and as long as the left arm remains connected and he fires from the inside toward the ball with the right foot, right knee, right hip and right shoulder—the harder he fires the farther he'll hit the ball, dead on line.

I stress the feeling of connected covering because a golfer who is having difficulty regardless of his ability level is invariably fighting some kind or kinds of disconnection which cause the player to drop the club (instead of springing the shaft) and drag the heel at the ball. From these beginnings, consistently squaring the face at impact is left to hand manipulation, and hand manipulation is the mother of inconsistency.

The final analogy I want to leave with you in regard to a feel sense for the firing of the right side is one that few students forget. Whenever a golfer coils into the brace of the right leg and drives off the inside of the right foot, this springing action of the legs, as I mentioned earlier, tightens all of the large muscles of the insides of the legs up through the posterior into the lower back. Imagine, just prior to initiating the change of direction with the kick of the right foot and right knee, that you had a dime "where the sun don't shine," that is, between the cheeks of your fanny. During the entire releasing action, clear to the finish of the swing, hold the dime! If you don't fire and shoot your balance immediately to the left foot, you're going to misplace some imaginary small change. The feeling should be identical to the one you experienced when you tried to smack the cart seat with connection.

COMMON DENOMINATOR 5

The golfer *must,* after initiating the change of direction with the right foot and right knee, immediately release the entire right side and center, insuring that the triangle returns to the original position squaring the club to the ball at impact.

COMMON DENOMINATOR 6

The golfer must, at waist high past the ball, have maintained the triangle with the belt buckle and center facing toward the target.

CHAPTER NINE

THE STRAIGHT BALANCED FINISH

A straight balanced finish is the living proof that a player has created and preserved his connections and that he has fired the right side and totally released center. By a straight balanced finish, I specifically mean that the golfer's knees, hips and shoulders are level, and that the weight has been entirely transferred to the left side at the completion of the swing. On the completed follow-throughs of the great ball strikers, you could draw a line from the left foot to the right shoulder, and that line is vertical or very nearly so.

Many golfers, particularly young players with flexible spines, hold center back and hit into the inverted "C" or bow position. As we discussed in our section on misleading terms, this often stems from a player's conscious effort to "stay behind" a shot, with the result that center is not released—it hangs back. When a player does this, he is hitting under and up instead of down and through the ball. In reality, the upper body is falling away from the shot. This is why a spectator will see so many duck hooks and fat iron shots at a junior tournament.

From our first analogy with the tossing of the shag bag, on through the operation of the triangle, the firing of the right side, smacking the chair, and "holding the dime," I have been trying to make sure the golfer understands that he or she must initiate the downswing with the feet and legs—from the ground up—and continue this sequential releasing with connection right up through center until ultimately the player has released the entire spine. Once we have coiled properly behind the ball, and fired the right side from the ground up, we are going to be in the proper position behind the ball at impact. We don't have to give it a second thought—it's done! Consciously trying to stay there only creates disconnection.

If we were to get extremely technical and take, perhaps, fifty high-speed sequence photos of one of the swings of the great ball strikers, we might actually find that center does stop for a milli-second during the early firing of the right side. Newton's law that "every action has an equal and opposite reaction" has to be in there someplace between the time the legs reverse and the upper body catches up and releases. But Newton's law is plenty—the worst thing you can do is make an intentional and incorrect attempt to improve upon it.

When I'm teaching the straight balanced finish, students will often ask, "Doesn't Nicklaus finish in an inverted 'C' or bow position?" The answer is, "Not when he's playing well." I also want to clear up a couple of other questions that arise in regard to the finish. Certain players are so flexible in the torso that, viewed straight on, they may give the appearance of completing the swing in the bow position. Their flexibility allows center to recoil even farther to the left, and consequently their left lat, left shoulder and left arm appear behind them, creating the illusion of an inverted "C". Study pictures of Weiskopf finishing and you will notice that a line drawn from the left foot to the right shoulder is absolutely vertical. From behind, it is obvious that the knees, hips and shoulders are absolutely level, and that the weight has been moved entirely to the left side. This is a straight balanced finish. Weiskopf has not laid back. On the contrary, because of his suppleness, center and the entire spine have been released a little farther than is the case in the swings of other great golfers.

**COMMON DENOMINATOR #7
The golfer must complete the swing with the knees, hips and shoulders level, and the weight entirely on the left side. The straight balanced finish is the proof that connection has been preserved throughout the swing.**

The straight balanced finish is the final evidence that you have created and preserved connection, fired the right side, and totally released your center into the shot. As in the likeness of Nelson, knees, hips and shoulders are absolutely level and weight has been transferred entirely to the left side.

Trying to "stay behind the ball" or achieve an "inverted 'C'" finish results in an incomplete transfer of weight and a tendency to swing up on the ball instead of down and through.

Byron Nelson

INCORRECT

Also, when a player finishes straight, balanced and level, there is some pressure in the legs, but there should be *no* pressure in the lower back. This is an excellent personal checkpoint. If you feel pressure in the lower back, it's almost a certainty that center has not been fully released. After finishing correctly, many fine players drop down and back slightly as they watch the shot, simply to take the pressure out of the legs. Hale Irwin and Jerry Pate sometimes do this. But it is simply an idiosyncrasy—when they're playing well, neither finishes in a position that is not straight, level and balanced.

Illustrations here and in the next chapter should convince you that the great ball strikers finish the swing in a straight balanced fashion. I would also like to remind you that connection and the straight balanced finish promote longevity. There has never been a player, to my knowledge, that played well for an extended period of time and finished in the bow or inverted "C" position. So do us both a favor, play better golf and avoid orthopedic surgery—arrive at the finish of your swing straight, balanced and level.

COMMON DENOMINATOR 7

The golfer must complete the swing with the knees, hips and shoulders level, and the weight entirely on the left side. The straight balanced finish is proof that connection has been preserved during the swing.

CHAPTER TEN

SUMMARY AND REVIEW OF THE SEVEN COMMON DENOMINATORS

This chapter provides a quick word-and-picture review of the seven common denominators and the inter-related connective elements of the full swing. Hagen, Nicklaus and Littler are featured here, but it could just as well be Jones, Hogan and Player, or Nelson, Snead and Trevino. The point is that all of the great ball strikers exhibit all of the essential fundamentals discussed throughout the book.

Let me stress again that there are differences in mannerism and style; that is, every golfer's swing has certain elements of individuality much like one's personality, profile or fingerprints. I have never seen two people walk the same way, let alone swing a golf club exactly as one another. Even with the tour's identical twins, Curtis and Allen Strange, with whom I've worked, there are perceptible differences in the way they handle a golf club.

One of the greatest dangers the average golfer faces is the tendency to adopt a mannerism because he sees a good player do it. He does this without either knowledge or regard for its relationship to the necessary fundamentals. Such an approach usually backfires, whereas incorporating the seven common denominators leaves you with your own swing, yet one that is truly sound.

COMMON DENOMINATOR 1

The golfer must create connection at the outset through a braced connected address position.

In the address position, legs are braced, knees knocked in slightly. The feet are spread to shoulder width, and the ball is played off the inside of the left heel. Weight is on the insides of the feet with the larger inside muscles engaged. There is the appearance in all three players of athletic, responsive comfort.

The triangle of arms and hands is intact, and the butt of the club points toward center of the chest.

Knees and hips are level. The right shoulder is under the left only because the right hand is placed under the left on the club. Nicklaus' right shoulder is a little lower because he sets his hands slightly forward.

The three players have avoided bending the spine forward. They measure to the ball by inclining the spine erectly from the hips. The center of the chest is "up" and all three appear "tall to the ball" in the address position. There is no perceptible tension in the shoulders, arms or hands.

WALTER HAGEN

JACK NICKLAUS

GENE LITTLER

COMMON DENOMINATOR 2

The golfer must begin the swing by taking the triangle and center away together.

To initiate the swing, all three players take the triangle and center away as a unit. At or near waist high, the hands, arms, connected shoulders and center all begin the coiling process. The arms never disconnect and "run off" the upper torso which is the common error among poorer golfers who often pick or lift the arms and retard center.

The picture of Nicklaus exemplifies a perfect connected takeaway. The fact that the hands have remained lined up with the center of the chest is proof positive that everything has moved away from the ball together. This is the true one-piece takeaway.

COMMON DENOMINATOR 3

The golfer must coil the triangle and center behind the ball into the brace of the right leg.

By continuing the connected coiling on the backswing, all three players have moved totally behind the ball so that the weight is loaded into the inside of the right foot, leg and the inside of the right hip joint. The head and the upper torso have moved to the right but none of these players has swayed.

As explained earlier, golf's most common disconnection is the sway forward or the reverse pivot. Unless the golfer coils as deeply as possible into the brace of the right leg, maximum potential cannot be reached.

COMMON DENOMINATOR 4

The golfer must reverse the club with the right foot and right knee to create the proper position at the top of the swing.

The position at the top is achieved with the reverse of the legs. The transition from the completion of the backswing to the start of the downswing is created by a kick of the right foot and right knee toward the ball. It is this move that creates the "fall-in" which sets the club on the proper downswing plane. The most common error made by the average golfer at this point is to literally reverse the process. That is, he initiates the swing with the arms and hands instead of the kick of the right foot and knee toward the ball. When this happens the club cannot fall into the desired inside plane, but must be thrown or cast out and over causing the club to approach the ball from the outside in.

(Note: The ideal position from which to view the change of direction is looking down the target line from behind the golfer. See the "shaft-springing" sequence of Tom Watson, page 114.)

COMMON DENOMINATOR 5

The golfer *must*, after initiating the change of direction with the right foot and right knee, immediately release the entire right side and center, insuring that the triangle returns to the original position squaring the club to the ball at impact.

Notice that in each of the illustrations the continued firing of the right side from the ground up and including center has recreated the triangle in the impact area with the hands and butt of the club pointing toward center. The positions closely resemble setup and the club, hand and center configuration, as seen through the re-emergence of the triangle, leaves no doubt that the club has been squared to the intended line of flight at impact. Understand that the club in each of these illustrations is traveling approximately 100 m.p.h. Here, the moment of truth has been reached perfectly because the correct application of the preceding four common denominators has created the causes necessary to produce the proper effect.

Most golfers fail to recreate this position because they have not coiled properly on the backswing, initiated with the kick of the right foot and knee, and immediately continued by the firing of the entire right side and center.

COMMON DENOMINATOR 6

The golfer must, at waist high past the ball, have maintained the triangle with the belt buckle and center facing toward the target.

At waist high on the follow-through the great ball strikers continue to release the body and center. Notice that the left arm begins to fold on the body as the right extends down the line.

If center had been retarded, the left arm would have disconnected from the left shoulder, "unplugged," and we would see a blocking action. Because of an insufficient coil on the backswing (reverse pivot) and /or the failure to fire the right side strongly and continue releasing, most golfers are unable to arrive at the position illustrated.

Notice also that all three players are behind the shot. This is not because they made a conscious effort to do so. It is because they coiled behind the ball on the backswing and initiated the forward swing from the ground up, in other words, by early compliance with the common denominators.

7 COMMON DENOMINATOR

The golfer must complete the swing with the knees, hips and shoulders level, and the weight entirely on the left side. The straight balanced finish is proof that connection has been preserved during the swing.

All three players have completed the swing in the straight balanced finish position. The weight has been completely transferred to the left side, so much so that each player could actually pick the right foot off the ground.

Remember, no player who has finished in the inverted or reverse "C" position has been competitively successful for a significant period of time. The inverted "C" finish position means that center has not been fully released and it has prematurely ended many careers because it invites lower back injury.

The connected swing, utilizing the larger muscles of the body, naturally leads to a fully released, level and balanced finish. From beginning to end, the connected swing incorporating each of the common denominators has promoted longevity in the games of the great ball strikers and I am convinced it will do the same for you. After all, golf is a lifetime sport and the ultimate purpose for those of us who love it is to play as well as we can for as long as we can.

TOM WEISKOPF:
Connection In The Short Game

Throughout this book, we have dealt with the fundamental elements of the full golf swing on all standard full shots. Obviously, there are numerous occasions when the golfer must attempt to consciously control the height of the shot (wind, obstacles, etc.) and the shape of the shot (intentional fades or draws, etc.). Also, there are myriad special short shots (chips, pitches, blasts, etc.) that the player needs to know to extricate himself from trouble.

A detailed discussion of these golf shots is beyond the scope of this book. But let me state here that:

1) any and all of these shots are governed by the elements of the seven common denominators , and

2) special shots require the pre-setting of certain angles but never a deviation from the rule that every shot must be the product of a connected swing, fully released.

Whether it's a hooded, door-high, 2-iron played back in the stance into the teeth of the wind, or, as in the exemplary Tom Weiskopf sequence presented here, a soft lob shot over a bunker played off the left heel, the necessary clubface angle must be pre-set, and then the swing must be made with the same connected releasing action we encountered in the study of the standard full swing under normal conditions.

1. Tom Weiskopf has pre-set the angle of his clubface to an open position in order to produce a high soft lob. His stance is slightly open, with the ball played approximately opposite the left heel.

2. Triangle and center have moved away together. Notice that his hands stay as a unit linked to the center of his chest, assuring uniform swing radius.

3. Notice the spectator "appear" behind his left shoulder. Tom's coil allows the body to move marginally and naturally to his right by way of the abbreviated backswing.

4. Minature kick of right foot and knee moves the balance point past the ball and changes the direction of the club.

5. At all times the triangle remains intact; here it reappears as Weiskopf releases the hands with the body returning the club to the pre-set open clubface position created at address.

6. As the body continues releasing, the left arm connection remains intact.

7. With full release, weight is completely on the left side. The right arm covers the left in the follow-through and hands remain lined up to the center of the chest. "Center" has been released completely, and head and eyes naturally come up to track the flight of the shot.

BEN HOGAN:
A Case History In Connection

In an actual lesson situation, following a thorough introduction of the common denominators, I make a point of discussing the differences in the "earlier" and "later" swings of Ben Hogan. I have found that this practice is both fascinating to students, and, more importantly, it provides a quick practical review which helps cement the understanding of a fundamental sound, connected striking action.

Normally, I will ask pupils what they think is wrong with the earlier swing. Without exception, they will mention that the club is far below parallel at the top— i.e. "an overswing." They will now recognize a left arm disconnection. In the old swing Hogan pulled the arms up *off* the chest, unplugging, and finished the backswing from the shoulder joint. In the new swing, the left arm and shoulder operate as a connected unit which took the club to the proper position at the top.

Also, the observer will notice a difference in weight distribution. In the old swing, the disconnection and drop left more weight on the left leg. Thus, in the old downswing we see a slight lowering of the head, and a sliding of arms in the hitting area. But in the new swing, the left arm has remained perfectly connected and the entire body, from the ground up through center, has been more fully released.

At the three quarter point in the follow-through, the old swing graphically illustrates the "blocking" action. The right arm is well under the left (notice the daylight between the arms) and the weight has not been sufficiently moved to the left side. From here, Hogan hit

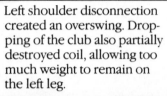

Left shoulder disconnection created an overswing. Dropping of the club also partially destroyed coil, allowing too much weight to remain on the left leg.

Disconnection causes slight drop of head and center arms pulling and sliding slightly across the body.

Result of disconnection: "blocking" action with the right arm under left, and "daylight" visible between the arms. Upper body and center are laid back.

Left arm and shoulder are now connected, with more weight coiled into the inside muscles of the right leg. Net result: stronger backswing position. Shorter swing, yet a longer arc has been created by the maintaining of connection and deeper coil behind the ball.

Left arm connection maintained perfectly, with the entire body more fully released from the ground up through center.

Right arm covers left as left begins to fold on the body. Right side and center have fully released, and weight is totally transferred to left side. Shoulders near the level position on the way to a straight balanced finish.

those low hooks he referred to as "the terror of the field mice."

In the new swing, notice that the right arm covers the left as the left begins to fold down on the body. The right side is fully extended, center is fully released, the weight has been completely transferred to the left side, and the shoulders are nearing level on the way to a straight balanced finish. In the old swing, Hogan was able, at times, to "block" the ball on a straight line because he always had near perfect foot and leg action. But, until he eliminated the disconnection, he never became a great ball striker. Once he did, he became, in the opinion of most, the best ball striker in the history of the game.